The Beat Must Go On

Reimagining Inclusion for a Divided Era

Nichole Barnes Marshall

Contents

Author's Note   5
In The Beginning (There Was Jack)   7

1. Bring Down the Walls   21
2. A Deeper Love   43
3. Move Your Body   59
4. Follow Me   77
5. Good Life   101
6. Feel The Drive   113
7. The Music Sounds Better with You   125
8. Promised Land   150
9. On and On   164
   Epilogue: The World House   177

Discography   188
About the Author   189

Author's Note

This book would not exist without the people who shaped both my thinking and my courage.

To my favorite DJ, my husband, Kenny: You have been my steady rhythm through every transition. Your belief in me and this project has sustained me through the toughest times. You are the perfect blend over a 4/4 beat. Thank you.

To my children Kennedy, Erin, and Nick: This book is for you, to help you prepare to navigate a world that is both more connected and more divided than the one I grew up in. You remind me daily why this work matters. I love you.

To my dearly departed grandparents, Mama and Uncle Bill, who raised me with the understanding that devotion to family and your community is not optional: Everything I know about creating belonging I learned first at home with you on the South Side of Chicago. Thank you.

Author's Note

To john a. powell, who directs the Othering & Belonging Institute at UC Berkeley: Your work on targeted universalism and belonging has profoundly influenced how I understand inclusion. Thank you.

To the culture leaders, DEI practitioners, and belonging architects still holding the line, and to those who were pushed out for doing exactly what you were hired to do: This book is for you. I see the courage it takes to defend work that shouldn't need defending, to keep showing up in rooms that are shrinking. This book celebrates your persistence and stands as proof that the work you've given your careers to is still needed for such a time as this. I see you.

To the House DJs, the ones who kept the beat alive for decades when the mainstream looked the other way: You taught me that the dance floor is the most inclusive space ever created, and that truth became the foundation of everything in these pages. This book exists because you showed the world what unity sounds like when someone has the courage to play it. Thank you.

And to every person who has ever felt like they did not belong, only to discover a dance floor, a community, a moment when they were finally, fully welcomed: This book is for you, too.

The beat goes on. And it goes on with all of us.

Nichole Barnes Marshall
Spring 2026

In The Beginning
(There Was Jack)
Building the World House

In the beginning, there was Jack, and Jack had a groove.

— Chip E., *Jack Trax*

In 1967, Dr. Martin Luther King Jr. wrote of the World House, the inescapable truth that we have inherited a large house, a great World House in which we have to live together. Black and white, Easterner and Westerner, Gentile and Jew, Catholic and Protestant, Muslim and Hindu. A family unduly separated in ideas, culture, and interest, who—because we can never again live apart—must learn somehow to live with each other in peace.

Nearly sixty years later, the need to build this prophetic house is more urgent than ever.

This book is my take on a construction manual for the World House—practical guidance from someone who has spent 25 years in the field, learning what works, and what does not, when you are trying to create spaces where everyone can belong.

Before I could become a builder, though, I had to learn what a house could be.

When the Beat First Found Me

It was a Saturday night in 1984, and I was about to discover something that would change my life forever, though I had no idea at the time. My cousin Will was supposed to babysit me at my mother's apartment, but the last thing a senior at Lindblom High School wanted to do was stay in on a Saturday night with his 11-year-old cousin.

With the sternest, I-mean-business grimace on his face, Will sat me down and said, "Look, I am going to take you out with me. You do not say anything to anybody. You do not leave my sight. You just hang out but be seen and not heard. Got it?" I got it.

Twenty minutes later, I heard it: a loud, rhythmic thumping that seemed to shake the car itself. Boom, boom, boom, boom. It was the loudest bass beat I had ever heard, so powerful I could feel it in my chest. My panic about being taken to someplace scary melted into excitement when I saw the sign: Chicago Mendel Catholic High School.

As we descended those dark stairs into what felt like another world, the muffled bass became a full groove that pulled me forward like gravity. And when we stepped into that room, everything changed. The music did not just hit my ears. I felt it on my body and in my soul. It was House music, and that night was my baptism.

Chicago is the birthplace of House music, and spaces like Mendel were a sanctuary; where Black and Brown and queer bodies moved together, where the DJ was a guide rather than a gatekeeper, where the only credential for entry was your willingness to surrender to the rhythm. I did not have language for it then, but I was experiencing belonging. Not *inclusion* as a corporate noun, sanitized and strategic. *Belonging* as a verb. As sweat and bass and the stranger beside you becoming bonded by the beat for four hours on a Saturday night.

There is a track from that era, a sermon set to synthesizers, that declared: "In the beginning, there was Jack, and Jack had a groove."[1] Jack was not a person. It was a way of moving. "To jack" was to let the music take your body, a dance style where you surrendered control to the beat and let it move through you. And from this groove came the groove of all grooves.

The groove was not just a sound. It was a philosophy. House music taught me that unity was not uniformity, that you could bring your whole self to the dance floor and still move together. When the beat dropped, nobody asked where you came from or what you did for a living or who you loved. The music either moved you or it did not.

What I witnessed was not just a party. It was something

---

1. Chuck Roberts with Rhythm Controll, "My House," Catch a Beat Records, 1987.

closer to church. People from different neighborhoods, different backgrounds, different everything, all moving together to a sound that somehow made perfect sense of all our differences. The DJ that night was the legendary Ron Hardy, one of the Godfathers of House, blending disco, funk, R&B, and even clips from Dr. Martin Luther King, Jr. speeches into something that felt holy.

I did not know it then, but I was experiencing the power of what happens when marginalized communities create spaces where everyone can bring their authentic selves. What I was feeling in that high school gymnasium would eventually guide my approach to building inclusive communities for the next four decades.

I was standing in the World House. I just did not have the words for it yet.

The foundation for that understanding was laid long before Mendel, in a three-flat on the South Side where my grandparents raised me along with more than twenty foster children, teaching me through sheer example that building community was not an abstraction but a daily practice. And the urgency behind it crystallized a few years later, when two men in an elevator at the University of Chicago looked at a thirteen-year-old Black girl and decided she did not belong. Those stories—the house that taught me to build, and the door that slammed shut in my face—shaped everything that came after. You will hear them both in the chapters ahead.

What followed was a career spanning more than two decades and some of the world's most recognized brands:

IBM, Tribune Company, Aon, L Brands, Bath & Body Works, Pinterest. I designed inclusion strategies that touched millions of employees and customers across the globe. I saw what was possible when organizations committed to belonging. I also witnessed the resistance, backlash, and confusion that accompany efforts to change who gets to be in the room. But for most of those years, I kept the professional work and the dance floor in separate compartments. I never imagined they belonged together.

When the Connection Finally Clicked

That changed in 2022, in a hotel room at one in the morning.

I was preparing for a company event where employees could conduct workshops on what personally inspired them. After years of keeping my House music passion private in professional settings, I had decided to lead a workshop on its history. After all, the event was in my hometown; it just felt right for me to do it. But it also felt risky. I worried that sharing this deeply personal part of myself would undermine my credibility as a leader.

But as I sat reviewing my research, I stumbled onto something that stopped me cold: the full story of Disco Demolition Night.

I had vague memories of it from childhood. I was about seven years old in 1979, and I remembered seeing images of the riot at Comiskey Park on television. But I had never understood what it really meant.

Steve Dahl, a rock radio DJ, angry that his station had switched to a disco format, organized a promotional stunt between games of a White Sox doubleheader. Fans were invited to bring disco records to be destroyed in center field. But what showed up in those crates was not just disco. People brought R&B records, soul records, gospel albums, salsa music. They brought anything associated with Black and Brown and gay communities. When they detonated the records, the crowd did not just cheer. They stormed the field. What was marketed as a celebration of rock music revealed itself as something far more disturbing: a violent rejection of the cultures that had created disco in the first place.

And then I read what happened next.

Disco did not die that night. It went underground. In Chicago, in Detroit, in New York, the communities who had created disco, soul, and funk took their music into basements and warehouses and lofts and high school gymnasiums. They kept those beats and blended in European electronic sounds, gospel rhythms, jazz grooves, Latin and Afro beats, and even industrial sounds like fast moving trains. Like gumbo, they mixed a lot of sounds from different cultures and created something entirely new.

It was House music. The name came from partygoers who had experienced Frankie Knuckles during his residency at The Warehouse nightclub. His 1977-82 residency earned him the title Godfather of House Music. He was renowned for playing obscure and rare tracks that could not be heard on the radio, so fans would go to their local record store (mine was Dr. Wax in Hyde Park) and ask for the "warehouse music", which over time became "House music." By 1984, Jesse Saunders had produced "On and On," widely regarded as the first House record. Forty years later, electronic dance music has evolved into a twelve-billion-dollar global industry that brings tens of millions of people together at festivals around the world.

I felt something unlock in my chest.

This was the story of DEI. This is what happens when marginalized communities face rejection and choose not to disappear. They innovate. They create something new from what they were told had no value. They build community around their authentic expression. And what they create ends up transforming the world.

I had been living this philosophy my entire life without naming it. Those Saturday nights at Mendel, Hales Franciscan, or my alma mater, Hyde Park High School, were not just parties. They were laboratories of inclusion, spaces where the principles I would later try to teach in corporate boardrooms were already being practiced on dance floors.

The DJ became my model for what inclusive leadership actually looks like. Not the leader who commands from above, but the one who reads the room, manages energy, and creates the conditions for collective joy without ever demanding that the room follow orders. The legends of House understood something most leadership books still have not figured out: the goal is not to be the center of attention. The goal is to make everyone else feel like they are. That model runs through every chapter of this book.

This book is the translation of everything I have learned, on the dance floor and in the C-suite, about what it takes to build spaces where everyone belongs. It is the completion of a journey that began when I was eleven years old, watching my cousin dance across a crowded gymnasium with the confidence of someone who knew exactly where he belonged. It is the merging of every part of myself I had kept separate for decades: the child who grew up in House culture, the professional who built a career in corporate America, the woman who learned that authenticity and credibility are not opposites.

House music built the blueprint. This book is the construction manual.

Where We Are Now: The Structures Being Dismantled

Today, the diversity, equity, and inclusion field finds itself at a crossroads. What was once embraced as essential progress toward a more representative democracy now faces significant backlash. DEI functions are being dismantled, programs are being defunded, and professionals like me are watching structures that transformed countless lives being systematically undone.

The numbers are staggering. According to gender economist Katica Roy, more than 300,000 Black women have lost their jobs in a single year, casualties of policies designed to punish those who dared to build bridges.[2] Chief Diversity Officers who were hired with fanfare after 2020 are being quietly let go or seeing their roles eliminated entirely. The very title of my profession has become politically toxic in some circles.

The current political climate has polarized conversations about inclusion to the point that nuanced dialogue feels nearly impossible. On one side, some see any acknowledgment of historical inequity or current disparities as divisive and discriminatory. On the other side, some view any criticism of DEI approaches as evidence of racism, sexism, or other forms of bias.

Both sides have retreated into echo chambers that amplify their perspectives while drowning out dissenting voices. What gets lost in this polarization is the practical wisdom that comes from actually doing this work, understanding both its transformative potential and its real limitations.

The dismantling is not just a policy shift. It is personal. It represents the undoing of structures that have created pathways of opportunity for generations previously excluded. When universities eliminate their diversity offices, the very programs that enabled my husband and many of our friends to attend, it is heartbreaking for those who chose these institutions specifically for their inclusive values.

But this moment also presents an opportunity. How do we

---

2. Katica Roy, "300,000 Black women have left the labor force in three months. It's not a coincidence," MS Now, July 17, 2025, https://www.ms.now/business-culture/300000-black-women-left-labor-force-3-months-s-not-coincidence-rcna219355.

move beyond defensive debates to build bridges of understanding? How do we acknowledge that while DEI work has not been perfect and has had unintended consequences for some, its foundational purpose remains vital in our increasingly interconnected world?

The answer, I believe, is to stop defending a field and start building a house.

A Word for the Skeptic

Maybe you picked up this book with doubts. Maybe you have heard that DEI is divisive, that it is about lowering standards, that it is a solution in search of a problem. Maybe you have seen programs that felt performative or trainings that made things worse. Maybe you are not sure any of this is worth saving.

I am glad you are here.

Some of the backlash against DEI work is legitimate. I have seen poorly designed programs that created more division than connection. I have witnessed performative gestures that accomplished nothing except to make executives feel good about themselves. I have experienced the frustration of being asked to put a diversity stamp on decisions that were made without any input from the people most affected.

If your skepticism comes from those kinds of experiences, I share it.

But I have also seen what happens when this work is done well. I have watched teams transform from dysfunctional collections of individuals into communities where everyone contributes their best thinking. I have seen organizations discover talent they had been overlooking for decades. I have experienced the relief on someone's face when they realize they can finally be themselves at work.

Maybe you have also heard that recent tragedies, like the fatal plane collision over the Potomac in January 2025, happened because of diversity hiring. Let me be direct: blaming DEI for unrelated failures is not skepticism. It is scapegoating. It is using tragedy to advance an agenda that was already written. That is not critical thinking. It is deflection.

True skepticism asks hard questions and stays open to evidence. If that is you, this book will give you plenty to consider. I will not ask you to accept anything on faith. I will show you what I have seen work and what I have seen fail and let you draw your own conclusions.

The door to the World House is open to skeptics, too. Just be willing to look around before you decide what you think.

The Music Is the Map

I named each chapter after a classic House music track because the songs hold the philosophy. Bring Down The Walls. A Deeper Love. Move Your Body. Follow Me.

Good Life. Feel the Drive. The Music Sounds Better with You. Promised Land. On and On.

If you know these songs, you will hear them differently after reading this book. If you do not know them, I invite you to listen. The groove has been teaching us how to build the World House for forty years. We just need to pay attention.

Each chapter builds a different step in the house-building process:

- Chapter 1 is The Demolition, where we tear down the myths and distortions that prevent us from seeing each other clearly.
- Chapter 2 is The Blueprint, where we develop the empathetic understanding that guides all construction.
- Chapter 3 is The Mobilization, where we learn to move people past resistance and into action.
- Chapter 4 is The DJ Booth, where we develop the skills to lead without dominating, to guide without controlling.
- Chapter 5 is The Infrastructure, where we design systems that connect rather than separate.
- Chapter 6 is The Foundation, where we honor the history we build on while creating something new.
- Chapter 7 is The Dance Floor, where belonging becomes possible because the structures support it.

- Chapter 8 is The Vision, where we see what the completed house could be.
- Chapter 9 is The Threshold, where you step from being a reader into a builder.
- And the Epilogue is The World House itself, the invitation to enter.

There are people working to build the World House, and there are people working to tear it down. This book is for the builders and anyone ready to become one.

In the beginning, there was Jack.

And Jack had a groove.

And now it is time to build.

Chapter 1
Bring Down the Walls
The Demolition

We're gonna bring down them walls, let 'em fall, fall, fall.

— Fingers Incorporated, "Bring Down the Walls"

Before you can build a house, you have to clear the site.

The World House we are constructing together cannot rise on contaminated ground. The myths we have inherited about who belongs and who does not, about what diversity means and what it threatens, about who deserves opportunity and who must earn it twice over—these are the debris we must remove before the foundation can be poured.

This chapter is about demolition: the necessary clearing that makes new construction possible. We are tearing down walls that were never meant to protect us—walls built from fear, misunderstanding, and the comfortable lies we tell ourselves about meritocracy.

The work is not gentle. But what we are making room for is worth it.

When the Music Stops

It was a rainy, gray day in September and annual budget discussions were in full swing with the HR leadership team. I had made the transition into a full-time DEI program manager from a seasoned IT recruiter who was successful at sourcing and hiring diverse talent in hard-to-fill roles. Being in my first DEI role symbolized a kind of progress that was aligned with my purpose. I did not have to be the second Black mayor of Chicago to make a difference. I could do that by ensuring all people, especially those most marginalized, could experience growth and dignity in their careers. And by doing so, I got to move up another rung on the corporate ladder and be in the room where it happens, where the most critical employee decisions are being made.

I was sitting in a glass conference room that felt like I was being curiously observed in a fishbowl, watching a heated debate unfold about employee resource groups. What had started as a conversation about budget allocation had devolved into something much more emotionally charged.

"These groups are creating division instead of unity," argued one executive. "They are making people focus on what separates us instead of what brings us together."

"That is not what they are for," responded another. "They

provide crucial support and networking opportunities for underrepresented employees."

"But what about reverse discrimination? Are we excluding people based on their identity now?"

Well, cue up Netflix, because I have starred in, critiqued, and watched this movie many times before. Well-intentioned people talking past one another, each side convinced they are right, everyone frustrated that the other side cannot see the obvious truth of their position. And here I am sitting in the middle, ready to advocate on behalf of the ERGs, while recognizing that the opposite view deserves to be heard. What became painfully clear to me was that there were several misunderstandings of the purpose of ERGs.

That conversation in the conference room was not the first time I had watched smart, well-meaning people talk past each other about who belongs and why. It was not even the hundredth. But every time it happens, I feel a familiar tightness in my chest, a muscle memory from long before I had a title or a seat at any leadership table.

Because before I learned to name these patterns, before I could stand in a room full of executives and calmly untangle their assumptions, I had to feel one land on me. And the first one hit when I was thirteen years old.

When Difference First Hurt

The summer before my first year of high school, my academic performance, including being named valedictorian of my elementary school, earned me a spot in an enrichment program at the University of Chicago. Two days a week, I would leave my entirely Black world in the Chatham neighborhood and enter Hyde Park, where I was suddenly surrounded by people from around the globe who did not look like me.

One day, leaving the Regenstein library with my yellow Sony Walkman and foam headphones, I entered an elevator with two older men. They probably thought I could not hear their conversation over my music. One whispered, "What is she doing here?" The other whispered back, "It must be Affirmative Action."

I was 13 years old. Up until that moment, my entire world had been Black. Black neighborhood, Black families, Black schools, mostly Black teachers, Black-owned businesses, Black churches, Black bus drivers. I was well-educated about Black history because so many of my teachers had lived through the Civil Rights Movement and were committed to teaching us our heritage, even if it was not in the formal curriculum.

But I did not fully understand what Affirmative Action was. What was crystal clear was that those two men did not think I belonged there. That somehow my age or gender or race, something completely out of my control, disqualified me from attending one of the top universities in the country.

That was the first time I felt the door of a house slam shut in my face.

By no means was this the level of violence and indignity my grandparents experienced growing up on sharecroppers' farms in the Jim Crow South, fleeing north for a chance at freedom. But I felt that first twinge of loss of personhood, that sense of not being good enough for no other reason than existing.

That experience put me on a path to a long career dedicated to ensuring that no one would be denied a chance to reach their full potential. That everyone, regardless of where they are from, what they look like, or who they love, would be treated with dignity and respect and given a chance to be great.

I decided then, though I could not have articulated it this way, that I would spend my life building houses where doors stayed open.

Why This Matters to You

It would take me years to understand what happened in that elevator. Not the words themselves, those were clear enough. But the invisible architecture behind them. The assumptions those men carried into that small space. The story they had already written about a Black girl in a university library before she ever opened her mouth.

I have spent the decades since then learning to see that architecture everywhere: in boardrooms, in hiring committees, in the way a leadership team debates ERG budgets without ever questioning the assumptions underneath the debate. The structures are not always as blunt as two men whispering in an elevator. More often, they sound reasonable. They sound like common sense. They sound like fairness.

That is what makes them so hard to demolish. I call them Diversity Distortions.

In the pages ahead, you will learn how to recognize the common Diversity Distortions that create resistance to inclusion efforts, understand the psychological reasons why otherwise intelligent, values-driven people often disagree about DEI, identify these patterns in your own thinking and conversations, and create conditions where productive dialogue becomes possible.

Think of it as learning to test the sound system before the music starts, making sure everyone can hear clearly before trying to get them to dance together.

The Diversity Distortions That Build Walls

After 25 years of doing this work, I have heard the same misconceptions surface again and again across different industries, companies, and communities. These are not necessarily malicious arguments. Many come from people who, either by privilege or choice, are unskilled in grappling with such complex issues. But like static on a radio, they interfere with clear communication and make productive dialogue nearly impossible.

Diversity Distortion #1: DEI is reverse discrimination that punishes White people for their identity.

This might be the most persistent Diversity Distortion I encounter, and I understand why it feels real to people who experience it. When you have been used to certain advantages, even if you did not realize they were advantages, equity can feel like a loss.

I saw this firsthand when I developed a global sponsorship program at a Fortune 500 company. The program paired high-performing employees from underrepresented backgrounds with senior executives who could advocate for their advancement. The goal was to address what research showed was a critical gap: women and people of color were over-mentored and under-sponsored, meaning they received plenty of advice but fewer opportunities for high-visibility assignments and career advancement.

The program requirements were rigorous. Participants had to be top performers who had completed a selective leadership development program. They underwent 360 assessments and cultural evaluations. The executives were carefully matched based on development needs and communication styles. This was about accelerating proven talent, not lowering standards.

Yet some colleagues still questioned whether it was fair. Were we excluding straight, cisgender, non-disabled white men from succession planning? No. Were they still being promoted into leadership positions? Yes. Did they still have access to C-suite mentoring? Absolutely. Was anyone actively excluded from career opportunities because of their identity? No.

But here is what was happening that critics could not see: informal sponsorship had always existed, on golf courses, during after-work drinks, through alumni networks, even in casual hallway conversations. Our program simply formalized and made transparent what had been happening informally for decades, while ensuring it reached talent that traditional networks had missed.

The program was incredibly successful. One hundred percent of participants said it was worthwhile. Some pairs created new products that the company brought to market. Three people found new roles through their sponsors. Employee engagement among participants was seven points higher than that of their peers at their level.

What I learned from this: When any person feels excluded from something, even something they never had access to before, it hurts and can look like discrimination to them. Feelings feel real, and dismissing them only amplifies defensiveness. Human beings are naturally loss-averse. We feel the pain of losing something more acutely than the pleasure of gaining something equivalent. When people hear about changing systems to be more inclusive, those who have succeeded in current systems often perceive that as a threat.

I believe many in the DEI community did dismiss those early negative reactions to our work as narrow-minded or bigoted, which contributed to the backlash we are experiencing today. This does not excuse those who condemned efforts like this because they believed the traditional archetype of leaders were more qualified based on their identity. But it does teach those of us who lead inclusion to practice it in how we hear opposition.

A more effective approach: Acknowledge the fear of loss directly rather than dismissing it. Help people understand that creating more pathways to success does not invalidate existing achievements; it just means more people get to achieve success as well. They will not lose a slice of the pie; the pie expands for more to benefit from it.

Diversity Distortion #2: We should be colorblind and treat everyone exactly the same.

This distortion seems fair and reasonable on the surface. Who could argue with treating everyone the same? But it represents a misunderstanding about how fairness actually works in practice and completely dismisses the fact that systemic racism is very real and that not one of us is truly colorblind.

While leading DEI for a global retailer, I observed this lesson up close. One of the marketing leaders engaged my team after a few missteps with global campaigns. A massive product launch using identical imagery, store layouts, and marketing messaging across varying international markets backfired when some audiences were put off, while others were responsive.

Another marketing campaign that felt welcoming to customers in the Midwest felt exclusionary to customers in Asia, not because the message was different, but because cultural context shaped how it was received. The same store layout that felt comfortable to customers in one community felt alienating to customers in another.

I understood the intent: to deliver a consistent message across markets based on past performance. Unfortunately, what was not understood was the impact. Not developing and testing the messages in those markets led to variable performance, reputational loss, and customer disengagement. What seemed like identical and fair treatment created very different customer experiences across different cultural contexts.

Treating everyone the same only works when everyone starts from the same place and has the same needs. But when people have different starting points, different barriers, and different cultural contexts, identical treatment often produces unequal results.

Aim for equitable outcomes rather than identical processes, like a good DJ who adjusts the mix based on the energy in the room. A great set cannot be ordered up like a Happy Meal; repeating the same songs in the same order in different environments misses the moment. Effective inclusion requires understanding your audience and adapting your approach accordingly.

Diversity Distortion #3: DEI strategies lower standards and compromise merit.

This distortion assumes that our existing systems are perfectly objective at identifying merit and that considering diversity somehow corrupts this pure process. My experience suggests the opposite is often true.

When I analyzed hiring data across multiple companies, I consistently found patterns that revealed how subjective the supposedly "objective" processes really were. Identical resumes received different ratings based on assumptions about the name at the top. The same leadership behavior was described as "confident" when displayed by men and "aggressive" when displayed by women. This allows biases such as affinity (favorability based on similar backgrounds and experiences), confirmation (favorability based on initial impression), or halo/horns (letting one perceived positive or negative trait determine the evaluation) to be accepted in leadership decisions such as hiring, firing, promotions, and performance evaluations.

At one company, my team discovered that the culture fit assessments were inadvertently screening out qualified candidates who did not match the cultural norms of our existing team, which was itself not representative of our customer base. When we redesigned our process to focus on culture add—what unique perspectives candidates could contribute—we not only improved diversity but actually hired more innovative and effective team members.

In my experience, and research suggests this as well, most White Americans do not see themselves as a distinct culture. They tend to generalize themselves as Americans or acknowledge their European ancestry, e.g. Irish American, Italian American, etc. However, the work of inclusion is rooted in cross-cultural competence, which posits that all humans are inherently cultural beings and we all belong to a culture.

So, when inclusion efforts suggest that White Americans are indeed a culture and their group has had unfair advantages, it can feel like an attack on their identity rather than a learning opportunity. I've heard statements like, "I've never oppressed anyone" and "No one ever gave me anything because I'm White."

During my time at various companies, I noticed that resistance to reexamining merit often came not from people who were objectively losing anything, but from people who felt their group membership was being devalued or criticized. This is not really only about policies or programs. It is about people's fundamental need to feel good about themselves and their communities. Effective inclusion work helps people expand their identity to include responsibility for their current and future actions rather than asking them to feel bad about who they are.

Well-designed inclusion strategies do not lower standards. They help us identify talent we were missing because our systems had unconscious biases built into them.

Diversity Distortion #4: DEI is just political correctness and virtue signaling.

I hear this critique often, and sometimes it is not entirely wrong. Some DEI efforts do focus more on appearances than substance, more on making organizations look good than creating real change.

I saw this happen a lot after the murder of George Floyd in 2020. Countless organizations sought to send a message of solidarity with their employees and consumers who expressed outrage at the dehumanization of Black lives. These efforts included everything from putting black boxes on their Instagram profiles to donating large sums to organizations supporting Black communities, signing pledges to hire more Black board members and executives, and hiring Black Chief Diversity Officers. It was a dizzying array of corporate engagement in Black life that left me with mixed feelings.

On one hand, as a Black woman having spent my entire adult life working in corporate America and knowing intimately the pain of exclusion, I was thrilled at the prospect of finally being seen. And as a DEI leader, this put my work at the center of the storm. For this moment in time, I was more than ready.

But then came the reckoning. The pledges made in the heat of 2020 began to fade. The Chief Diversity Officers who were hired with fanfare found their budgets cut and their influence diminished. And when the backlash came, when DEI became a political target, many of those same organizations retreated faster than they had previously advanced.

What I have learned from this whiplash period is that performative inclusion is actually worse than no inclusion at all. It raises expectations only to dash them. It creates cynicism that makes future efforts harder. It gives ammunition to critics who say the whole enterprise is just theater.

The World House is not built with press releases. It is built with policies, processes, and persistent attention to who gets included in what and who does not.

Sometimes resistance to DEI comes from this simpler place: people feel overwhelmed by complex terminology, competing frameworks, and conflicting information about what they are supposed to do or think. I have seen brilliant executives shut down in diversity learning courses not because they opposed inclusion, but because they felt ignorant or inadequate when faced with unfamiliar concepts and language. That defensive feeling then gets misinterpreted as resistance to the values themselves. When the loudest version of inclusion work looks performative, it is easy to dismiss the whole project.

There is a real difference between performative gestures and strategic inclusion. Rather than focusing solely on the shiny objects, I focused on tried and true methods of culture change: integrating equitable processes and inclusive practices into the systems where business and talent decisions are made and driving accountability for those efforts from the top. Meet people where they are. Use language they can connect with. Focus on results rather than appearances.

Diversity Distortion #5: DEI is divisive and creates separation instead of unity.

This concern often comes from people who have experienced poorly implemented diversity strategies and policies that were perceived as divisive. I have seen employee resource groups that became echo chambers, training sessions that made people feel attacked rather than educated, and policies that seemed to pit different groups against each other.

But I have also seen what happens when inclusion is done well. There was one company whose employee resource groups became some of their most effective vehicles for cross-cultural learning and collaboration. Rather than segregating people, they created bridges between communities that had previously been isolated from each other.

The key was ensuring that these groups were not just safe spaces for similar people to gather. They were also platforms for sharing perspectives, building alliances, and working together on challenges that affected everyone.

Unity does not require uniformity. Like those House music parties where people from different backgrounds came together around shared love of the music, true community can accommodate differences while building around common purposes.

How the Walls Get Built

Nobody wakes up one morning and decides to misunderstand inclusion. That's what makes Diversity Distortions so persistent: They don't feel like distortions to the people holding them. They feel like common sense.

I've worn glasses for the majority of my life and need them to see anything beyond my arm's reach. And for all those who are tethered to their glasses, you know they can get dirty pretty easily. Some people are very disciplined about cleaning their glasses regularly. They use wipes or a cloth, even their shirttail or a napkin, anything to keep their vision clear. Others can have visible spots, lint and fingerprints on their glasses and be totally unbothered.

I've sat across the table from thousands of smart, accomplished, caring people who metaphorically looked at the world through dirty glasses. Not because they were unwilling or unable to clean them. Because they never thought they needed to.

It is important to understand that most distortions are born in isolation. When your neighborhood, your office, your dinner table, and your news feed all look and sound the same, you're not hearing the full track. You're hearing one loop on repeat and mistaking it for the whole song. You don't know what you're missing because you've never heard it.

Then layer on the noise: The headlines that reduce decades of systemic inequality to a tweet. The political talking points designed to generate heat, not light. The algorithm feeding you outrage, because outrage keeps you scrolling. People aren't forming their views about inclusion in a vacuum. They're forming them in a wind tunnel of incomplete, oversimplified, and often deliberately distorted information.

Now add experience. Someone sat through a diversity training where they were told they were the problem before anyone bothered to learn their name. Someone watched a hiring decision that felt like it prioritized optics over excellence. Someone raised a concern and got labeled resistant. Those experiences leave marks. And one bad experience with inclusion work can become the lens through which every future effort gets judged, the same way one terrible DJ set can make you swear off a whole genre of music.

And underneath all of it, our own wiring works against us. The brain is a confirmation machine. It hunts for evidence that supports what we already believe and quietly discards the rest. Once a Diversity Distortion takes root, your mind will curate a highlight reel of proof that it's true and filter out everything that says otherwise.

So here's what you're actually dealing with: isolation, noise, wounds, and wiring. Four forces that have nothing to do with character and everything to do with conditions.

That distinction matters. Because if you think distortions come from bad people, your only move is to fight them. But if you understand they come from bad conditions, you can change the conditions.

And changing conditions? That's what a great DJ does every single night.

From Diversity Distortions to Understanding

Sometimes I think about that girl in the elevator. Thirteen years old, foam headphones around her neck, yellow Walkman clipped to her hip. She did not have a framework for what happened to her that day. She did not have the language of Diversity Distortions or the decades of professional experience that would eventually teach her to name what she felt. She just knew that something had broken, that the world had revealed a door she did not know existed by slamming it shut.

I will never know whether those men were acting from ignorance or conviction. Maybe they had never examined their assumptions about who belongs in a prestigious university library. Maybe they had, and simply did not believe a Black girl from the South Side qualified. What I know is that the impact was the same. The door slammed shut either way.

And what I have learned since is that most walls are built by people who never examined their blueprints, and some are built by people who knew exactly what they were constructing. I have sat across the table from leaders who genuinely did not understand how their systems excluded people. I have also sat across from leaders who understood perfectly well and decided that exclusion served their interests. Treating those two realities as if they are the same is its own kind of distortion, and it lets deliberate harm hide behind the benefit of the doubt.

This book focuses on the walls that can come down—the ones held up by distortion rather than malice—because that is where most people are, and where the most movement is possible. But I want to be clear about something: choosing to focus there is not the same as pretending the other walls do not exist. The people who have been deliberately excluded, pushed out, passed over, and harmed by design deserve to have that truth named plainly. Their experience is not a misunderstanding to be cleared up with better dialogue. It is an injustice that requires accountability.

One of the important things I have learned over my career is that demolition is not destruction. You do not tear down walls to leave people standing in the rubble. You tear them down to make room for something better. But you have to be honest about what you are tearing down and why, or the new construction will not hold.

So where does that leave us? With a choice about where to aim. The way forward starts with shared values, not because everyone shares them, but because enough of us do. Most people, regardless of their position on specific DEI practices, care deeply about fairness, opportunity, excellence, and community. When I begin a difficult conversation by finding that common ground, I am not being naive. I am being strategic. I am doing what every great DJ does before dropping a new track: meeting the room where it is, so I can take it somewhere it has never been.

It also requires leading with stories rather than statistics. Data matters, and we will get to it throughout this book. But the conversation in that conference room shifted because I told a story that made the numbers feel human. Stories do not trigger the same defenses that data does. They slip past the confirmation bias and land somewhere deeper.

And it demands that we acknowledge legitimate concerns without flattening them. When someone worries about reverse discrimination, they might be expressing a real fear about fairness, even if their understanding of the situation is incomplete. When someone says DEI feels divisive, they may be describing a real experience with a badly run program. Dismissing those concerns does not make them disappear. It drives them underground, where they harden into resentment. But acknowledging them does not mean accepting them uncritically, either. It means being willing to stay in the conversation long enough to separate the fear from the fact.

Most of all, it requires us to focus on what is possible. I have spent enough of my career debunking myths. The more powerful move is to paint a picture of what the world looks like when inclusion works, when teams are stronger because they think differently, when companies grow and innovate because they finally see the talent they were stepping over or the ideas they were dismissing, when communities hold together because everyone has a stake in the outcome.

That thirteen-year-old girl in the elevator could not have imagined any of this. She could not have known that the sting of that moment would become the engine of her life's work, or that she would one day stand in rooms full of the most powerful people in corporate America and help them see what they had been missing. She did not yet know that some of those rooms would hold people who wanted to do better, and others who had no intention of changing. She just knew it hurt. And she decided, in a way she could not yet articulate, that she would spend her life making sure fewer doors slammed shut, whether they were closed by carelessness or by design.

The demolition is not the end. It is the clearing. And now that we have examined the rubble and understood what built these walls in the first place, we are ready for what comes next: the blueprint.

Because a great DJ does not just clear the floor. A great DJ reads the room, feels the energy, and knows exactly what song to play next to bring everyone back together. That is Chapter 2. And the music is about to change.

Chapter 2
A Deeper Love
The Blueprint

Pride, a deeper love, a deeper love inside.

— Clivillés and Cole, "A Deeper Love"

Every building starts with a blueprint. Before the foundation is poured, before the walls go up, before anyone can move in, someone has to envision what the structure will be.

The blueprint for the World House is empathetic understanding—the deep comprehension that comes from listening to experiences different from your own.

This chapter is about learning to draw that blueprint. It is about developing the kind of listening that hears not just words but the meaning beneath them. The kind of curiosity that seeks to understand before seeking to be understood. The kind of connection that makes it possible to build something together.

The title comes from the song that reminds us: Deeper love requires real listening. And real listening is harder than it sounds.

When I Learned to Hear

While leading DEI at one of my prior employers, I was facilitating what I thought would be a straightforward discussion about our global diversity strategy. The room was filled with leaders from across our international offices: London, Hong Kong, Sao Paulo, Johannesburg. On paper, it looked like exactly the kind of diverse leadership team that should be easy to align around inclusion goals.

Ten minutes in, I realized I was completely wrong.

Our leader from London was politely but firmly explaining that their approach to inclusion was quite different from the American model. Our Sao Paulo representative was frustrated that we kept talking about race in binary terms that did not reflect the spectrum of diversity by skin color, which is the Brazilian reality. The Hong Kong team was concerned that family-focused benefits might conflict with their performance culture. And everyone seemed to be talking past each other, using the same words to mean different things.

I had fallen into the trap that catches so many of us in this work: assuming that because we all cared about inclusion, we all understood it the same way. I was trying to conduct an orchestra where every musician was reading from a different piece of sheet music.

The kind of leadership needed here is like what elite DJs did. The best DJs did not just play music. They listened to the room. They paid attention to how people responded, what was working, what was not, and adjusted accordingly. They understood that the same track could move a crowd or clear a dance floor depending on the timing, the context, and whether people felt ready to receive it.

I stopped talking and started listening.

When the Gap Becomes a Mirror

I teach people about unconscious bias for a living. I have facilitated hundreds of workshops helping others recognize the assumptions operating beneath their awareness. I have coached executives through their defensive reactions when their blind spots are revealed.

None of that prepared me for the moment my own bias fell out of my mouth in front of the very community I thought I was serving.

I was at a Cubs game in a hospitality suite my company had sponsored for an LGBTQ organization. We were hosting the event as a pro bono fundraiser, demonstrating our commitment to the community. I was there as a representative of our DEI function, surrounded by community members and organizational leaders.

The conversation turned to parenting and how difficult it is to raise children in an environment where so much adult content is available online. My daughters were young at the time and had just started exploring YouTube. I mentioned a cartoon I had seen that contained sexualized content clearly targeting children. The cartoon featured two male superheroes in bed together.

As the words came out of my mouth, I heard myself emphasizing the wrong thing. The real issue was age-inappropriate sexual content being marketed to children. But what I was expressing concern about was that it was two men in the bed.

I saw the faces of the people I was talking to change. The unspoken question hung in the air: What is wrong with two men in a bed?

No one needed to say anything. I started arguing with myself internally. I had grown up watching *The Brady Bunch*, where Carol and Mike shared a bed on network television. That was groundbreaking for its time, but no one suggested it was harmful for children to see a heterosexual couple in bed together. Why was I reacting differently to this?

The answer was uncomfortable: I had a bias I did not know I was carrying. Somewhere in my mind, I had absorbed a belief that same-sex relationships required special explanation, that my children needed to be prepared before being exposed to them in a way they did not need to be prepared for heterosexual relationships.

I knew instantly what had happened because I taught this material. But knowing the theory did not prevent me from experiencing the reality. My filter was dirty, and it had just contaminated a conversation with the very community I was supposed to be supporting.

I do not know if I lost credibility with those community members that day. No one confronted me directly. But I know I lost credibility with myself. I had to reconcile my stated beliefs with the belief that had been operating in the background, influencing my reactions without my awareness.

I started sharing that story in workshops after that. Not to excuse myself but to demonstrate something important: Even people who do this work professionally carry biases they have not fully interrogated. Even well-intentioned people say things that reveal assumptions they did not know they held. The verbal faux pas is not necessarily evidence of deep-seated hatred. It is evidence of beliefs that have gone unexamined.

What matters is what happens next. Do you acknowledge the harm? Do you get the education you need? Do you take intentional steps to examine and address the bias? Do you change your behavior going forward? Emphatically yes, yes, yes, and yes.

I cannot undo what I said that day. But I can use it as a teaching moment, both for others and for myself. I can stay vigilant about my own filters. I can approach every conversation knowing that I still have blind spots I have not discovered yet.

This is what it means to do the inner work of inclusion. Not to achieve some perfect state of bias-free enlightenment but to commit to the ongoing practice of catching yourself, examining yourself, and growing from what you find.

Why This Matters to You

Whether you are leading a team with different cultural backgrounds, trying to have a productive conversation with family members who see the world differently, or facilitating any discussion where people's experiences and perspectives vary significantly, this chapter is about developing the listening skills that make connection possible.

You will learn how to move beyond surface-level politeness to deep understanding across difference, create psychological safety where people can share authentic perspectives, navigate conversations where the same words mean different things to different people, and build the kind of trust that enables productive dialogue about difficult topics.

Think of it as learning to be a DJ who can read any room and create the conditions where everyone feels included before asking them to move together.

When Listening Became Leadership

That meeting at work became a turning point, not just for our diversity strategy but for my understanding of what authentic leadership across differences requires. Instead of pushing forward with my prepared agenda, I did something that felt risky at the time: I admitted that I was missing something important.

"I am hearing that we are all using similar language but meaning different things," I said. "Before we can align on strategy, I think we need to understand each other's realities better. Would you be willing to help me learn what inclusion looks like in your region?"

What happened next transformed not just that meeting, but how our entire global team worked together.

Our London colleague explained that in the UK, class background often mattered more than race in determining access to opportunities, and that American-style ethnic categories did not capture the complexity of British diversity. The Sao Paulo team described a context where economic inequality intersected with race in ways that made simple demographic targets irrelevant. Hong Kong shared how generational differences between local employees and expatriate leaders created inclusion challenges that our standard frameworks could not address.

Instead of trying to force everyone into the same model, we began designing approaches that honored different cultural contexts while working toward shared goals. The strategies we developed were more sophisticated, more effective, and more sustainable than anything I could have created from my American corporate perspective alone.

Authentic listening does not just make people feel better. It makes the solutions better.

The Music Theory of Empathetic Connection

Years later, when I was enjoying a "House at the Plaza" midday House party in downtown Chicago, I realized something I hadn't expected. I had been thinking about DJs—how they read the room, how they lead. But the real revelation was about the dance floor.

Because the magic of a House party doesn't just happen in the DJ booth. It happens in the bodies and minds of every person in that space. On this day, there were about a thousand people filling up Daley Plaza in the middle of the work week, on their lunch breaks, with their full attention fixed on DJ Steve "Miggedy" Maestro. What that audience was doing, what *we* were doing at all those day parties, festivals, even the night-to-daybreak party marathons, without knowing it, was practicing one of the most sophisticated forms of listening there is.

Think about what happens when you're on a dance floor and the music is right. You're not passively receiving sound. You're actively searching for something inside it. Your ears are tracking the bass line while your body responds to the rhythm and your mind is already reaching ahead, wondering *Where is this going?* There's a curiosity in it that borders on hunger. You want to be surprised. You want the DJ to take you somewhere you didn't expect. But you also want those moments of recognition, when a familiar melody surfaces inside a new mix and your whole body says, *"Yes, that's my JAM!"* and the joy of the known and the unknown existing in the same groove. As I write, I'm viscerally reliving the moment when Steve played the disco anthem by Loose Joints, "Is It All Over My Face," and the eruption when he dropped the sound for the Chicago-style call-and-response, "Hell yeah!" Yes, the smile is still all over my face.

And then there's the anticipation. Anyone who has ever been on a House music floor knows the feeling: the DJ starts building. The layers accumulate. The energy rises. You can feel the crescendo coming in your chest before it arrives, and the entire room leans into it together, hundreds of strangers sharing the same held breath. When the beat finally drops, the release is collective. It moves through the room like a wave, and for that moment, everyone is synchronized. Not because anyone told them to be, but because they were all listening deeply enough to have the same feeling at the same place and at the same time.

That's not passive. That's not casual. That is a room full of people practicing radical attentiveness, to the music, to the energy, to each other.

Now think about what that kind of listening requires. It requires curiosity, the desire to encounter something unfamiliar and be changed by it. It requires patience, the willingness to let the build happen without rushing to the resolution. It requires vulnerability, the openness to be moved, to let something outside yourself shift something inside yourself. And it requires trust, the faith that if you stay present and keep listening, the journey will be worth it, even if you don't know where it's going.

These are exactly the skills that empathetic connection across difference demands: The ability to show up in a conversation with curiosity about what you might discover. The patience to let someone's story unfold without jumping ahead to your response. The vulnerability to let someone's experience touch you, even when it challenges what you thought you knew. The trust that staying in the discomfort of not understanding will eventually lead somewhere meaningful.

The dance floor taught me to listen before I ever learned the word *empathy*. And it taught me that the best listening isn't about waiting for your turn to speak. It's about wanting—truly wanting—to hear something you've never heard before.

The Anatomy of Authentic Listening

After years of facilitating difficult conversations across differences, I have identified specific skills that make empathetic connection possible, even in challenging circumstances.

Skill 1: Cultivating Curiosity

The foundation of empathetic listening is curiosity about other people's experiences and perspectives. Not the kind of curiosity that is just waiting for your turn to talk or looking for ammunition to prove your point but the curiosity that comes from recognizing that every person's experience contains wisdom you do not have.

During my years in the tech industry, I once worked with several teams that included employees who had immigrated to the US as adults. In our discussions about career development, I kept hearing concerns that did not make sense to me based on my own experience as a Black American woman who had navigated similar corporate environments.

Instead of assuming I understood their challenges, I asked them to help me learn. What I discovered was that their concerns about being seen as too ambitious or not humble enough reflected cultural norms from their countries of origin that I had never considered. Once I understood this context, we could design development programs that honored their cultural values while helping them navigate American corporate expectations.

Ask questions that come from a real interest in learning rather than from trying to prove a point or gather ammunition for your argument.

Skill 2: Listening for Values, Not Just Positions

When people express strong opinions about inclusion topics, they are usually not just sharing policy preferences. They are expressing deeply held values about fairness, community, opportunity, and belonging. Learning to hear the values underneath the positions creates opportunities for connection even when people disagree about specifics.

I saw this during a heated discussion at one of the retailers about our marketing campaigns. Some team members felt our ads should feature more diverse models to reflect our customer base. Others worried that forced diversity in marketing would feel inauthentic and hurt our brand.

Instead of getting stuck debating whether our current ads were diverse enough, I asked people to share what they loved about our brand and our relationship with customers. What I heard was really inspiring: personalizing every customer's experience, crave-worthy products, fun store atmosphere, fast and friendly checkout. These were shared not as a regurgitation of sales training, but how they felt as employees *and* customers of the brand.

Then I asked what values those elements represent. Inclusion, innovation, curiosity, efficiency, joy.

Once we identified these shared values, it put us at a much better starting place to begin designing campaigns that honored everyone's concerns, featuring diversity that felt authentic rather than forced, and ensuring that all our customers could see themselves reflected in our brand.

People who disagree about tactics often share underlying values. Finding those shared values creates a foundation for productive problem-solving.

Skill 3: Managing Your Emotional Reactions

Empathetic listening requires developing the ability to stay emotionally regulated, even when you hear things that trigger strong reactions. This does not mean suppressing your emotions. It means not letting them drive your responses in ways that shut down dialogue.

I had to develop this skill during a particularly challenging conversation at one company about our diversity hiring goals. One senior leader expressed concern that we were lowering our standards to hit demographic targets. Remembering that first experience of being belittled based on my identity at University of Chicago, and countless other indignities throughout my career, I felt a flash of anger and hurt.

My instinct was to respond defensively, to share my own experiences with having my qualifications questioned, to present data about bias in hiring processes and the lack of representation at the people leader level and above. Or I could wow him with all the McKinsey research about how much more profitable and productive diverse teams are. Any of those responses would have been valid, but would it actually change that leader's mind, or would it shift his focus towards my defensiveness? Another angry Black woman.

Instead, I took a breath and asked, "Help me understand what you mean by standards. What are you concerned might be compromised?" This uncovered a lot of assumptions and revealed the cognitive dissonance between this leader's beliefs and practices. Thankfully, their openness to feedback and guidance yielded a productive conversation about how we define merit, what our current hiring process might be missing, and how we could ensure both excellence and equity in our selection decisions.

Your emotional reactions contain important information about your values and experiences. But leading with those reactions can prevent the learning that is necessary for real change to occur.

Skill 4: Creating Safety for Difficult Truths

People can only share authentically when they feel safe from judgment, attack, or punishment. Creating this safety requires explicit attention to the conditions that make vulnerability possible.

During my time at one of the retail brands, I facilitated a session about workplace inclusion with a group of managers. Early in the conversation, one manager shared that he sometimes felt like he could not say anything right when it came to diversity topics and that he had started avoiding interactions with employees from different backgrounds to avoid accidentally offending someone.

His confession created a moment of tension. Some participants looked uncomfortable with his admission. Others seemed to be judging him for it. How I responded would determine whether the rest of the conversation would be honest or performative.

"Thank you for being honest about that," I said. "I imagine that is not an easy thing to admit, and I am guessing you are not the only person who has felt that way." Then I asked for a show of hands of who else had ever felt the same. Nearly the entire class raised their hand. When we avoid each other out of fear, nobody wins. I built upon that new comfort in the room to walk them through how to create conditions where everyone feels confident engaging across differences.

This response did two things: it validated his courage in sharing something vulnerable, and it framed his concern as a shared problem we could solve together rather than a character flaw to be criticized.

People need to feel safe being imperfect to be authentic. Creating this safety often requires explicitly normalizing the messiness of learning across differences.

One very important note before we go further. These listening skills are ones I've developed over 25 years as a professional facilitator and culture practitioner. I share them because educating people is my job. In the workplaces and organizations where I've been hired to lead change, I take on that responsibility willingly. But I want to be clear: *It is not everyone's responsibility to educate people who are uninformed or misinformed about this work.* Especially not the people who have been marginalized or underrepresented by the very systems we're trying to change. That burden has been placed on those communities for far too long, and I won't add to it here. What I will say is that these are powerful skills to have in your back pocket, and how and when you choose to use them is entirely up to you.

The blueprint is taking shape. You are learning to listen in ways that reveal what people actually need, not just what they say they want. You are developing the empathetic understanding that guides all construction.

But understanding is not enough. In the next chapter, we will learn how to mobilize that understanding into action, how to move people past resistance and into the work of building together.

The architect has drawn the plans. Now it is time to gather the crew.

Chapter 3
Move Your Body

The Mobilization

It's gonna set you free.

— Marshall Jefferson, "Move Your Body"

A blueprint without builders is just paper.

The World House requires mobilization, getting people off the sidelines and into the work. Not through force or guilt, but through the irresistible invitation of something worth building together.

This chapter is about learning to move people. To inspire them to contribute their energy and talents to something larger than themselves. In the same way that Marshall Jefferson's track moved bodies onto dance floors across Chicago, you will learn to create the conditions where people cannot help but join in.

The lyrics say it all: It is gonna set you free. And freedom is contagious.

Inclusion Starts from Within

Before I could lead inclusion, I had to understand how I responded to exclusion.

I grew up in what I call a "Rice Krispies" family because they would snap, crackle, and pop about anything. There was always a lot of loud talking in my grandmother's house. The laughs were full-bellied and raucous, and if you crossed the line, you were met with that same energy, just as intense, but definitely not fun. I felt as though I was always navigating a spectrum. On one end was lively debate and smack-talking expressiveness, which, as a softer-spoken kid, I later came to enjoy and got really good at holding my own. On the other end, that energy could escalate into yelling, fights, and corporal punishment that, even days after, would hang over me like a personal dark cloud.

I hated the dark side of the spectrum. I tried to avoid it at all costs. Something about the volume and intensity felt out of control and grated against my sensibilities as a child. The other kids didn't seem to be affected by it as much as I did. It almost felt like I didn't belong, even when I knew I was deeply loved and cared for.

One day, when I was maybe nine or ten years old, my grandmother, mother, and aunt got into a shouting match about something involving money. I had been sent to the back room, as children were, but I could hear them going at each other through the walls. The arguing escalated until I could not take it another second.

I stormed into the living room. "You need to stop it," I said. "You need to stop yelling at each other."

My aunt stopped mid-sentence, walked right up to my face with her long, red fingernail pointing at my forehead and said, "Go back in that room. You're a child. Stay in a child's place."

There it was again. Be seen and not heard. Stay in your place. I was being molded for silence and conformity. That generational conditioning that's been passed down since the plantations.

I did not remember that incident consciously for years. But it lived in my body. From that point forward, I stayed away from conflict. If people were about to argue, I would remove myself from the situation or, better yet, learn to diffuse it before it escalated. I became skilled at redirecting conversations, minimizing tension, smoothing things over before anyone got upset.

These are useful skills. They make you a good diplomat. They serve you well as a DEI leader who needs to navigate charged conversations without getting emotionally pulled into the vortex. But underneath those skills was something less healthy: an avoidance of anything I perceived as conflict, a belief that any negative emotion meant something had gone wrong, and a habit of shrinking my own voice to keep the peace.

I did not realize I had lost my voice until I was well into my adult career, still shrinking in moments of tension, still treating other people's authority as more legitimate than my own, still believing that my job was to make everyone else comfortable, even at the cost of my own authenticity.

The transformation happened gradually through years of DEI practice. I studied instructional design. I learned about unconscious bias, not just as a concept to teach others but as something operating in my own mind. I developed content for managers about giving constructive feedback. I facilitated difficult conversations about race and gender and identity. I managed employee resource groups without formal authority, learning to influence through listening rather than control.

My toolbox expanded from just avoidance to an extensive collection of approaches for navigating human complexity. And somewhere in that process, I began to heal.

I realized that "bad" was a label I was assigning to situations, not an objective truth about them. A difference of opinion was not inherently harmful. Conflict did not have to mean someone was being hurt. I could assert my own agency without accepting someone else as an authority over my voice. I could be present in difficult moments without being consumed by them.

The real test came during a video call with a senior executive at one of my prior employers. I had been trying to get time with him to discuss integrating DEI learning into an important company event. He had agreed in principle, but our meeting kept getting delayed. As the date neared and still no meeting, I escalated to my manager, his executive team peer, to help secure the time.

When we finally connected, I could tell he was furious. He believed I had misrepresented him as unsupportive of DEI work, that I was imposing content rather than collaborating, that I had gone over his head to push my agenda.

As I presented my recommendations, I watched him become more and more agitated. His breathing grew heavy. His eyes widened. And then he exploded.

He yelled at me. He demanded to know how I dared make assumptions about his commitment. He went on a tirade while I sat there, watching his face fill the video screen.

In that moment, I felt the old response rise up in my body. The "stay in your place" programming activated automatically. Everything in me wanted to shrink, to apologize, to make myself smaller until the storm passed.

But I had new tools now. I had learned to separate my emotional reaction from my response. I had practiced staying present in difficult conversations without getting pulled into the other person's emotional state.

So I let him finish. I kept my face neutral and attentive. I did not interrupt or defend myself. When he finally stopped, still breathing heavily, I let a moment of silence hang in the air.

Then I said, with all the care I could muster, "Thank you for sharing your thoughts. I've heard what you had to say. I'm sure it must feel threatening to think that I misrepresented you. That certainly was not my intention. My goal remains to achieve what our CEO asked me to do, which is to ensure all employees understand that inclusion is a priority and provide the learning that supports it. Why don't we take a pause and come back to the conversation when clearer heads can prevail?"

It did not calm him down. If anything, my composure seemed to frustrate him more. He ended the call abruptly.

But I did not spiral. I did not convince myself that my career was over, that I had ruined everything, that I needed to start looking for a new job. Instead, I called my manager, documented what had happened, clarified my goals, and kept moving forward.

I got my content into that event. The work my team and I developed is still being used today. That executive eventually took credit for it all. In the words of Whitney Houston, "It's not right, but it's OK. I'm gon' make it anyway."

What mattered most to me was that I did not shrink. I found my voice not by becoming louder or more aggressive but by using the skills I discussed in the last chapter: listening for values without absorbing someone else's emotional chaos; responding from intention rather than reacting from fear.

Because of that shift, I remained focused and achieved the goal. The work got done exceptionally well, and it made such a difference that the person who initially showed up as an obstacle became a champion (the toxic behavior of taking credit for another's work remains a separate issue).

So how do you transform resistance into real engagement and partnership? The answer lies in an experience I call "The Miraculous Conversion."

When Resistance Becomes Partnership

Early in my career, I encountered a leader who taught me everything I needed to know about mobilizing resistant allies. We will call him Dave, and he was one of the senior executives at a company where I was introducing employee resource groups (ERGs) into the company culture.

The company was headquartered in the far northern suburbs of Chicago, about thirty miles from the Wisconsin border. Beautiful campus. I will never forget walking into Dave's office on the executive floor for the first time. He was powerful, intimidating, much older than me, and much taller than me, and I am pretty tall. On his desk sat a photograph of him with President George H.W. Bush. The walls were covered with pictures of politicians and statesmen. I remember thinking: I am just a young Black girl from the South Side, and I cannot relate to anything in this man's world.

I had been warned about him. Dave's a tough customer, people told me. When you go talk to Dave, it is pretty much Dave's show and you are just in it.

But I had an audience with him, and I intended to use it.

The women's ERG had identified a problem they wanted to solve. Women at the company felt double-taxed, carrying full workplace responsibilities while still bearing most parental duties at home. Men had access to informal networking opportunities: drinks after work, golf outings, casual relationship-building that advanced careers. Women with children could not participate.

Similarly, other groups expressed concern about the distant work location being a barrier to attracting more diverse talent from the city, as well as issues with timeliness due to Chicago's notoriously heavy and unpredictable traffic, and no public transportation options extending to the area. One of the engineering divisions had recently opened a satellite office in downtown Chicago to solve for these issues, and several ERGs began lobbying for the company to purchase additional office space there for more flex-work options for city-based employees. This was long before Covid-era work-from-home technology became the standard.

I had all the data on employee attrition, where the glass ceiling and cliffs were for women's advancement, what the demographic mix was of employees that commuted more than 20 miles to work and presented all of this along with my recommended actions to Dave. He sat back in his big leather chair, arms folded, giving me that stern look I suspect he used to intimidate everyone. When I finished, he said, "Didn't these employees know where our office was when they took the job? Everyone seems to be looking for special treatment these days. Why can't they just do their jobs?"

It felt like a provocative trick to see if I'd take the bait. I pushed back. "I imagine that the workplace is very different than it was when you were early in your career. More mothers could stay at home with their children because a family could thrive on one good salary. And good jobs were probably easier to find closer to home. Given our company goals, we need to have an unfair share of the best talent in the marketplace. And while these strategies carry a price tag, it will never be more than what we gain in retention, productivity, and engagement, which all lead to growth, innovation, performance. Would you agree that's something we could use more of?"

I was so proud of myself for flipping the script with him. The conversation ended cordially, but he gave me no indication of whether he was swayed by my argument or not. I left that meeting feeling like I had completely wasted my time.

Months later, Dave's assistant came to find me. She informed me that he wanted to be an executive sponsor for the ERGs and support this work.

I do not know exactly what shifted for him. I had been locking in his peers as executive sponsors, so I'd like to think either my argument was that compelling, or he had FOMO and didn't want the optics of being uninvolved. Or maybe something in his personal life caused a change of heart. Sometimes there is a moment in the world that cracks something open. Sometimes the seed you plant just needs time to grow. What I know is this: Before I left the company, they had shifted their policy on working from home and flexing between campuses. They expanded the Chicago office footprint specifically to attract talent.

And one of the last things I did before I left? I walked in the Chicago Pride Parade with Dave at my side. Mr. George-Bush-picture-on-your-desk. Right there on the parade route, showing up for employees in a way he likely never would have considered a few years earlier.

That is what moving people off the sidelines looks like. It is rarely a single conversation. It is rarely a dramatic moment of conversion. It is showing up, making the case, standing your ground, and then, sometimes, if you are lucky, watching someone's heart change in ways you never could have predicted.

Here is what that experience taught me about mobilization: Resistance is not a wall. It is information. When someone pushes back, they are telling you something about what they fear, what they value, what they need to feel safe. If you fight the resistance, you confirm their fears. If you listen to it, you might find a path forward hiding behind the objections.

The question is never, *How do I defeat this person.* The question is: *What are they protecting, and how can I help them protect it while still moving forward?*

That reframe changes everything. It turns adversaries into collaborators. It turns obstacles into design constraints. It turns the people most likely to undermine your work into the people most invested in making it succeed.

Beyond Counting Heads: The Metrics That Actually Matter

There's a phrase I often used to succinctly describe the difference between diversity and inclusion: Diversity is counting heads; inclusion is making heads count. While I recognize how important metrics are to mobilizing conviction and alignment, all too often counting heads is the full data story of what the experience of working or serving in an organization looks and feels like—as if naturally having more diversity would yield more inclusion.

Early in my career, I measured success the way many organizations still do: by counting heads.

I started in DEI in the early 2000's as a recruiter, operating under a simple theory of change: If we hire more diverse talent, the culture will improve by virtue of bringing different people in. Increase representation, and inclusion will follow.

It is a seductive argument because it is easy to measure. You can track demographic percentages, set targets, and report progress in quarterly dashboards. Leadership understands headcount. Boards can evaluate whether numbers went up or down.

What I learned over decades of practice is that diversity without inclusion is a revolving door. And diversity and inclusion without belonging eliminates the value of walking through that door. I would recruit exceptional talent from underrepresented backgrounds and they would leave within eighteen months. The people already in the workplace did not have the skills or demonstrate the behaviors that made those new hires feel valued and appreciated. We were counting heads, not making heads count.

Representation matters. But representation alone tells you who is in the building. It does not tell you whether they are thriving, contributing, advancing, or planning their exit.

The Metrics That Changed My Approach

Over time, I shifted focus from representation to engagement, and specifically to the components that drive it.

I adopted the *"Say, Stay, Strive"* engagement framework, a model developed by Aon and widely used across industries.

- **Say** captures what employees express about the company and their managers. Do they speak positively about their workplace to friends and family? Do they recommend the organization to others? Or do they quietly warn people away?
- **Stay** measures commitment. Are employees actively engaged with their work, or are they scrolling job boards and taking recruiter calls? Retention statistics tell part of this story, but engagement surveys can surface flight risk before it shows up in turnover data.
- **Strive** is the element most organizations undervalue: discretionary effort. This is the

willingness to do one extra thing—to stay late on a project, to help a colleague who is struggling, to think creatively about a customer problem rather than defaulting to standard procedures.

Here is what research, and my own experience, confirmed: On average, employees give roughly 60 percent of their potential at work each day. That 60 percent covers the basics. It ensures the direct deposit arrives, the badge works at the door, the computer login functions. It is the minimum required to maintain employment.

The remaining 40 percent is discretionary. Employees choose whether to contribute it based on how they feel, not what they are paid.

For organizations seeking growth, innovation, or transformation, that 40 percent is the difference between adequate and exceptional. And you cannot mandate it. You cannot incentivize it with bonuses alone. You have to earn it by creating conditions that make people feel they belong.

What Drives Discretionary Effort

The data is remarkably consistent on this point. Discretionary effort flows from feelings, specifically feelings of belonging, contribution, autonomy, and meaningful connection.

When employees feel their manager cares about them, they give more effort. When they trust their team will support them, they take creative risks. When they believe their contributions matter, they invest themselves more fully.

This is why manager effectiveness became a central metric in my approach. People do not leave companies. They leave managers. A brilliant employee with a terrible manager will disengage, then depart. A struggling employee with an exceptional manager often finds their footing and flourishes.

We measured not just overall engagement but how engagement varied across different demographic groups. Not only by race and gender, but tenure, level, department, generation. If a particular department or function reported significantly lower belonging scores than the others, that was a signal. If Black employees rated their belief in the company's direction significantly lower than their white peers across functions, that revealed a pattern requiring deeper understanding.

The breakdown of the results told the real story. An organization can have strong aggregate engagement scores while specific populations are struggling. If you only look at the average, you miss the people falling through the cracks.

When Accommodation Becomes Engagement

At a company's distribution centers, production managers were flagging what they saw as a performance problem. Several Muslim employees were leaving the floor at specific times during their shifts. It looked like abandonment of work. It was disrupting production targets. Peers were confused. Managers were frustrated. The employees were being written up.

When my team was brought in, we heard the managers' perspective first. We understood why they were concerned. In distribution centers, every second is tracked. Every movement is measured. Ten minutes off the line can mean missed deadlines and unhappy customers.

But when we dug deeper, we saw something different. These employees weren't abandoning their work. They were trying to observe their religious obligations, the daily prayers required of practicing Muslims. There was no designated space for prayer, so they were going into bathrooms and hallways. The prayer times were interfering with their break schedules. They hadn't communicated what they needed because they didn't feel they could.

This wasn't a performance issue. It was an accommodation issue.

We reframed the conversation entirely. We facilitated meetings between the employees, their managers, and business leaders. We worked to understand exactly what observance required, which turned out to be less than ten minutes of prayer time at specific intervals. We identified spaces that could be designated for prayer. We worked with scheduling to ensure adequate coverage during those brief windows.

The solution required everyone at the table. We needed the employees to articulate their needs clearly. We needed managers to understand that accommodation wasn't about giving special treatment; it was about enabling employees to bring their full selves to work. We needed operations leaders to think creatively about coverage and scheduling.

What struck me was how simple the actual accommodation was compared to the conflict that had built up around it. Ten minutes. A designated room. A predictable schedule. That's all it took to transform employees who felt their jobs were in jeopardy into employees who felt seen by their employer.

The response from employees was overwhelming. Emails, calls, recognition—all expressing gratitude, not just for the practical solution but for the fact that someone had listened. The company they worked for had cared about what they needed.

From an engagement standpoint, that mattered. When employees can say "My company understood what I needed and found a way to support it," that's belonging. That's the difference between showing up to earn a paycheck and showing up because you want to contribute to something that values you.

The difficult conversation in this case wasn't with the employees. It was with leaders who had defaulted to viewing difference as disruption. Once we could help them see the same situation through a different lens, not "Why are these employees creating problems?" but "How do we create conditions where all employees can succeed?" the solution became obvious.

This is what I mean when I say DEI work must be anchored in reality. The accommodation didn't compromise productivity; it enhanced it, because employees who feel seen work harder than employees who feel surveilled. But we couldn't get there by lecturing managers about inclusion. We had to understand their concerns about production targets first, then show them how accommodation served those goals.

What Looks Good on Paper Versus What Captures Real Change

Some metrics are performative. They make organizations look good in press releases without reflecting lived experience.

Representation in hiring is one example. A company can trumpet that 40 percent of new hires last year were women, while ignoring that women are leaving at twice the rate of men. The front door is open, but the back door is revolving.

I learned to look at representation across the employee lifecycle, not just entry points. What does representation look like at each level of the organization? How do promotion rates compare across demographic groups? Who is leaving, and how long did they stay?

Engagement surveys can also be misleading if you only read the headlines. An organization might report 80 percent favorable engagement, while burying the fact that indexes on belonging or manager support show double-digit gaps between demographic groups or leaders or tenure.

The metrics that matter are the ones that reveal differential experience. They show you not just how the organization is doing but how it is doing for everyone. They surface the gaps between stated values and lived reality.

And they require courage to examine honestly. When the data reveals that your culture works better for some people than others, you have to be willing to act on that information rather than explain it away. A good crew chief, or any other inclusive leader, wouldn't have it any other way.

The crew is assembled. People are moving from the sidelines to the work site. The resistance that seemed immovable is beginning to shift.

But mobilization alone is not enough. In the next chapter, we will enter the DJ booth, the place where leadership happens. You will learn to guide without controlling, to create energy without forcing it, to help everyone find their part in the rhythm you are building together.

Chapter 4
Follow Me

Why don't you follow me/To a place where we can be free.

— Aly-Us, "Follow Me"

Every great dance floor has a DJ booth. A place where someone watches the whole room, reads the energy, and makes decisions about what happens next.

But the best DJs do not dominate. They guide. They create conditions where everyone can express themselves while contributing to something shared. They know when to turn up the energy and when to let the crowd breathe. They lead by serving.

This chapter is about learning to lead from the DJ booth. Not by commanding people to move, but by creating the conditions where they cannot help but join in. Not imposing your rhythm but helping everyone find theirs within a larger groove.

The title comes from the track that says, "Follow me to a place where we can be free." Real leadership in inclusion work is not about power. It is about liberation.

The DJ as Leader

For the World House, every construction site needs a crew chief. And in the World House, the crew chief is the DJ.

If you've never watched a great House DJ work, you might think they're just playing songs. They're not. They're leading. They're reading a room full of strangers and making hundreds of real-time decisions about what this particular crowd needs at a particular moment. They're managing energy, knowing when to push and when to pull back, when to surprise and when to give people exactly what they expect. They're creating the conditions for something they can't force: collective joy.

That's leadership. Not the kind you learn in most business schools, built on authority, hierarchy, and control, but the kind that emerges when someone takes responsibility for an entire room's experience without ever demanding that the room follow their orders.

Think about it. A CEO stands before a company and has to unify thousands of people around a shared mission while honoring that each person brings something different to the work. A manager sits with a team and has to draw out contributions from people with different strengths, different communication styles, different reasons for showing up. A community organizer walks into a neighborhood and has to build trust across generations, histories, and competing priorities, without a budget, a title, or the power to make anyone do anything.

The DJ does all of this. Every night. With nothing but two turntables and a crate of records (or a zip drive).

The legends—Frankie Knuckles, Ron Hardy, Larry Heard—understood something that most leadership books still haven't figured out: The goal isn't to be the center of attention. The goal is to make everyone else feel like they are. The DJ booth is elevated, not so the DJ can look down on the crowd, but so the DJ can see the whole floor. The position is one of service, not supremacy.

When Ron Hardy dropped a track at the Music Box, he wasn't performing for the crowd. He was performing *with* them. He watched their bodies, felt their energy, and responded. If the floor needed intensity, he gave them intensity. If they needed a moment to breathe, he pulled the energy back. If someone on the edge of the room hadn't found their rhythm yet, he'd shift the groove until they did. He never left anyone behind.

That's the leadership model this book is built on. The leader who guides from within. The leader who creates conditions where every person's unique contribution makes the whole thing better. The leader who builds a dance floor, not a following.

Throughout this book, the DJ will be our guide for what inclusive leadership looks like in practice. Every principle I've learned about creating belonging—in boardrooms, in communities, in organizations of every size—maps back to what I first witnessed in that gymnasium at Mendel High School. The DJ reads the room the way an empathetic leader reads their team. The DJ builds energy the way a skilled organizer builds a movement. The DJ blends different sounds into one groove the way a great CEO weaves different perspectives into a shared vision.

The turntables are a metaphor. But the leadership is real.

The Science of Connection

My favorite definition of connection comes from Brené Brown, who says "Connection is the energy that exists between people when they feel seen, heard, and valued; when they can give and receive without judgment; and when they derive sustenance and strength from the relationship."[1]

Many people can have the title of leader without having the ability to connect. And what we need to build the World House will require the will and skill to establish and maintain connections across differences. Some leaders leave people feeling heard, understood, and energized to work together. Others leave participants frustrated, defensive, and more convinced than ever that *those people* just

---

1. Brené Brown, *The Gifts of Imperfection: 10th Anniversary Edition* (Hazelden Publishing, 2022).

do not get it. The difference is not random. It is based on specific elements that either facilitate or hinder authentic dialogue across differences.

Recent neuroscience research reveals something fascinating: When people feel truly heard and understood, their brains synchronize.[2] The neural activity in the speaker's brain begins to mirror in the listener's brain, not just in language processing areas, but in emotional and empathy centers as well. This creates what researchers call a shared mental state, where understanding transcends mere information exchange.

But this synchronization only happens under certain conditions. The brain's threat detection system must feel safe. When people feel judged, dismissed, or attacked, their amygdala activates, shutting down the areas responsible for complex thinking and empathy. No meaningful dialogue can happen when brains are in defensive mode.

This is why so many diversity conversations go sideways. It is not that people are unwilling to connect. It is that the conditions for connection have not been established. You cannot synchronize with someone whose brain is treating you as a threat.

So what creates those conditions? What allows brains to

---

2. Michael Platt, et al., "Using Neuroscience To Create High-Performing Teams," Wharton@Work, Wharton School, University of Pennsylvania, January 2023, https://executiveeducation.wharton.upenn.edu/thought-lead ership/wharton-at-work/2023/01/synchrony-creating-high-performing-teams/.

feel safe enough to open, to synchronize, to truly connect across difference?

The answer is trust. And trust, it turns out, is more specific than most of us realize.

The Foundation Beneath Connection

I recently had the privilege of interviewing Dr. Rachel Talton, an award-winning strategist, executive coach and researcher whose work on trust transformed how I understand what makes connection possible.

Trust, Rachel taught me, is the willingness to be vulnerable. That is it. Not confidence that everything will go well. Not certainty that you will not be hurt. The willingness to be vulnerable anyway, to show up without armor, to share what you really think, to let yourself be seen.

"When I trust you, I trust you with my life," Rachel explains.[3] "I'm willing to be vulnerable with you because I know you have my best interest at heart. But here's the thing—if you were a person without morals, without a North Star, my trust in you could turn into something that hurts me. The willingness to be vulnerable leaves you wide open to be hurt as well as to be healed."

That distinction, hurt or healed, is why trustworthiness matters. You have to work at being trustworthy. It is not automatic.

---

3. Rachel Talton, Personal conversation with the author, [DATE OR YEAR].

But trust is not one singular act. It has three components, and all three must be present for that willingness to emerge.

Benevolence

"When I think about benevolence, I think about my grandmother," Rachel says. "My grandmother had nineteen children—no twins. She was just an angel. She used to wake up at four-thirty every morning singing Amazing Grace, cooking and washing and cleaning. I knew she had my best interest at heart. Always."

Rachel pauses. "But as much as I love my grandmother, I would not trust her to do my taxes."

I laugh because I know exactly where she is going.

"She only finished the eighth grade," Rachel continues. "Brilliant, yes. Nineteen brilliant children. But she didn't have the education, the tools, the resources, the experience, the exposure to do my taxes. That's the second dimension of trustworthiness: competence. Do you have the abilities, the experience, the expertise to do the job placed before you?"

Competence

This is the insight that changed how I think about trust in organizations. You can trust someone 100 percent in one area and not trust them at all in another. Rachel's grandmother was the embodiment of benevolence. No one could question her love or her commitment to her family's well-being. But benevolence alone does not make someone trustworthy for every task.

"When you're thinking about your direct reports, your leaders, your stakeholders," Rachel explains, "ask yourself: In which ways do they trust you? In which ways are you earning their trust?"

Most leaders focus on demonstrating competence. They want their teams to trust that they know what they are doing. But Rachel's research shows that in diverse environments, benevolence is often the missing piece. People from historically marginalized groups have learned through experience to be skeptical of whether organizations and leaders really care about their wellbeing. They have seen too many "initiatives" (I use quotation marks because all too often our work is labeled as an *initiative*, which is merely the start of an effort, not a fully formed and integrated strategy) that were really about appearances; too many leaders who said the right things but did not follow through.

Building trust with employees, constituents, and communities requires demonstrating benevolence through consistent action over time. It cannot be performed. It cannot be announced in a memo or promised in a town hall. You can only build the reality of it, one kept commitment at a time.

Integrity

The third element is integrity. But Rachel defines it differently than most people expect.

"Usually when I say integrity, people think high moral standards—honesty, transparency. But integrity in the context of trustworthiness is about shared values. Let me give you an example."

"If you and I were in the mafia," she pauses here for effect, "and we were colleagues, I might ask you to do something completely outside of your normal moral standards. But it meets the mafia's standards. And I know 100 percent that you're going to do that thing because we have shared values within that context."

It is a provocative example, but it illuminates something crucial. Integrity is not just about being a good person. It is about alignment. Do you share the same values as the people who are deciding whether to trust you?

In organizational contexts, this means employees are assessing whether their leaders actually share their values —not just stated company values, but lived values. When a leader says the organization values work-life balance but emails at midnight expecting immediate responses, there is a values gap. When a company claims to value diversity but promotes the same demographic profile over and over, there is a values gap. Those gaps erode trust, regardless of how competent or well-meaning the leader appears.

Psychological Safety: The Enabler

"Now," Rachel says, "psychological safety is different. It's the enabler of trust and trustworthiness. If you're a trustworthy person, you create a culture of trust, whether at home or at work. But people also need to feel psychologically safe. That means no retribution if they come to you and say, 'I have concerns about our direction,' or 'I feel I'm being overlooked.' They should feel completely safe, not just physically, not just emotionally, but psychologically safe, to share those things with you."

She brings it home: "Without trust, you can't have belonging. You can have diversity—you just count people up. But you cannot create belonging without trust."

This is why everything else in this book matters only if trust exists. You can have the frameworks, the programs, the stated values. But if people do not feel psychologically safe, if they do not experience their leaders as trustworthy—benevolent, competent, and sharing their values —then all the structures in the world will not create belonging.

Trust is the foundation beneath the floor we are trying to build.

Why This Matters for Leadership

This framework changed how I lead.

Before I understood it, I focused on being competent: having the right answers, running efficient meetings, delivering results. I assumed that if I was good at my job, people would trust me.

But competence without benevolence creates compliance, not connection. People will do what you ask because you have authority, not because they believe you care about them. And the moment your authority wavers, the moment the volume gets turned down, that compliance disappears.

Benevolence without competence creates affection but not confidence. People may like you, but they will not follow you into difficult territory because they are not sure you can get them through it.

And neither competence nor benevolence matters if your integrity is in question. If people have seen you say one thing and do another, every future promise is suspect. Trust is hard to build and easy to shatter.

The leaders who create real connection, the ones whose teams will follow them through the valleys, who will keep playing even when the stands are empty, are the ones who demonstrate all three. They show they care through their actions. They prove they are capable through their results. And they build a track record of consistency that makes their word mean something.

This is what it means to lead from the DJ booth. Not commanding the room through force but earning the room's trust through demonstrated trustworthiness. Creating the conditions where brains feel safe enough to synchronize, where people feel willing to be vulnerable, where real connection becomes possible.

The science tells us what connection requires. Rachel's framework tells us how to create it. The rest is practice.

Leading When the Music Gets Turned Down

My husband Kenny, or DJ Kenny B as many know him, had a DJ residency at a club on the ground floor of a high-rise condo building. Every time he turned the volume past five, the owner would walk over and shush him. Keep it down. The neighbors are complaining. It became known as the quiet place, a dance club where the music could never really breathe.

But Kenny is good. Really good. And people kept coming. They packed that floor even with the volume low, because what he was doing with the music transcended the decibels. Word spread. The crowd grew. And eventually, that crowd started demanding more sound. They wanted what they knew he could give them if only he was allowed to give it.

The owner noticed something important: the room was full. The register was full. The quiet place was working despite its limitations, which meant it could work even better without them.

So he invested in soundproofing. Upgraded the walls, sealed the gaps, did what was necessary to let the music exist at full volume without disturbing the neighbors. And then Kenny could really play. The restrictions that had defined the space eventually gave way because the quality of the work created demand that changed the conditions.

That story is a blueprint for this moment.

Right now, the volume on inclusion work is being turned down. Organizations are being shushed. The neighbors are complaining. Leaders who were ready to play full sets are being told to keep it at five, or lower. Some venues are shutting down entirely.

The question is not whether this is frustrating. It is. The question is what you do when the volume gets restricted.

You keep playing. You prove the value. You let the quality of the work create demand that eventually changes the conditions.

Because this is a cycle. And cycles, by definition, turn.

Our country has been here before. We had Reconstruction, real progress toward multiracial democracy. Then came Jim Crow, decades of violent retrenchment. I remember my family telling me about all of the political assassinations in the 1960s: Medgar Evers. JFK. Malcolm X. RFK. MLK. How they thought we would never get out of that valley. But out of that valley came the passage of the Civil Rights Act of 1964 and 1968, the Voting Rights Act, and the Immigration and Nationality Act. These set the stage for an era of expansion of civil liberties that our nation had never experienced. Now we find ourselves in another valley, watching an administration and movement dedicated to dismantling what was built.

But the pattern teaches us something important: we come out of valleys. Every single time. The organizations, the people, the institutions that stay engaged during the valley are the ones that emerge stronger when the cycle turns. The ones who abandon the work, who stop playing because the volume got restricted, have to start over from scratch when the soundproofing finally goes in.

This is what leadership looks like in difficult seasons. Not panic, not retreat, but persistence, with clear eyes about what is actually happening.

Smoke and Mirrors

What I am seeing right now are leaders giving preemptive compliance. Organizations so afraid of being targeted that they are eliminating everything with "DEI" in the name: gutting programs, renaming functions, stripping language from websites. Pivot and protect. And it is driven by fear, not law.

No laws have been passed that prohibit what we do. Executive orders are not legislation. Court challenges are ongoing. While the legal landscape is shifting due to the SFFA v. Harvard decision and others,[4] it is less conclusive on illegality of DEI than the headlines suggest. But fear does

---

4. "Summary of the Supreme Court's Decisions in Students for Fair Admissions v. President and Fellows of Harvard College ('SFFA v. Harvard') and Students for Fair Admissions v. University of North Carolina," Lawyers' Committee for Civil Rights Under Law (2023), https://www.lawyerscommittee.org/wp-content/uploads/2023/08/LC_Har vard-UNC-Cases_D.pdf.

not wait for clarity. Fear runs ahead and surrenders territory that was never actually under attack.

Meanwhile, the reality of our workforce, our marketplace, our world has not changed. We still interact across differences constantly. Every global supply chain, every diverse customer base, every multigenerational team requires people who can bridge differences effectively. That is cultural competence, a leadership skill. It was always a leadership skill. It got inappropriately segregated from leadership development and put into DEI because of the pressure to perform, to show we checked boxes, to virtue signal that organizations were doing the right thing.

But business does not exist solely to prove they are doing the right thing. Should they operate morally, ethically, responsibly? Yes. But businesses, institutions, and communities also cannot grow without it. Period.

That is what makes this moment almost absurd. As much as some seek to create their idealized society, wherever there was actual growth in history—wherever there was expansion or innovation or discovery—there were people who had to take in different ideas, connect across borders, and work together with people who did not look or think like them. The Silk Road was not built by people who only traded with their neighbors. The Renaissance was not sparked by artists who refused to learn from other cultures.

For many years in DEI workshops I shared the story of the monumental success of the Ford Taurus in the 1980s and '90s, of how its dominance in the automobile market was a result of Ford being the first to incorporate insights from everyday people into the vehicle's design: the stay-at-home mom, the travelling salesperson, the delivery driver, the factory worker, even folks who didn't drive. Imagine the perspective from those who only listened to industry experts and insiders. I'm sure they thought the design team was wasting time and money. But every leap forward in human history required someone to reach across a line they were told not to cross.

What Survives the Cycle

The organizations that are going to make it through this moment are the ones that start with values—not DEI labels, but actual values. What does this organization believe? What does it stand for? What kind of culture do we want to build, regardless of what we call it?

Then they examine the gap between stated values and lived experience. They address that gap systematically, using whatever language makes sense for their context. The work does not require a particular vocabulary. It requires honesty about whether your culture works for everyone or only for some.

Cultural competence—the ability to communicate, negotiate, and collaborate across difference—is agnostic of any particular identity. It is not exclusive to any group. It is human work, period. And organizations are still doing it. The tools remain relevant. In fact, they are more relevant now than ever, precisely because the environment has become more charged.

Resistance to inclusion often reveals an assumption that opportunity is zero-sum: if someone else gains, I must lose. But inclusion is not a political position. It is a business reality. The demographics are what they are and will only become more diverse until the difference is the mean. The markets are what they are and will only continue to mirror the values of its diverse marketplace. The talent pool is what it is and organizations that are winning the war for talent will continue to differentiate themselves through culture and opportunity. Leaders who understand this will outlast leaders who do not.

The Arc and the Work

Dr. King reminded us that the arc of the moral universe is long, but it bends toward justice. Even when those in power have no interest in that arc, our work continues to bend it. Every conversation that deepens understanding. Every system that gets redesigned to work for more people. Every leader who chooses to stay engaged rather than retreat.

And perhaps we needed something like this moment to prompt honest evaluation. What in our previous approach was actually working? How did we define performance? What needs to evolve? How do we continue bending the arc when the headwinds are fierce?

House music itself was born from exactly this kind of moment, when disco was declared dead, when the records were burned, when the culture was told it had no value.

The communities who loved that music did not disappear. They went underground and created something new—something that outlasted every critic and every backlash and every attempt to silence it.

That is the lineage we carry into this work.

The cycle will turn. It always does. The crowd will demand more. The conditions will change. The sound-proofing will go in.

The question is whether you will still be on the floor when the volume comes back up.

Leading When Tensions Rise

Authentic dialogue across differences inevitably produces moments of tension when perspectives clash, comfortable assumptions are challenged, or the conversation feels stuck. These moments often hold the most potential for learning, but only if we navigate them skillfully.

Rather than rushing to resolve tension, we can learn to see discomfort as information. It often signals that we are at the edge of our understanding, in what educators call the "learning zone." The key is to distinguish between produc-tive discomfort that leads to growth and destructive conflict that shuts down dialogue.

At one company, I witnessed what becomes possible when a leader moves from advocacy to collaboration in a time of crisis and what happens when that collaboration is cut short.

After the murder of George Floyd in 2020, many companies rushed to performative gestures to signal a commitment to inclusion but without a meaningful infrastructure to sustain it. I felt confident that what my team and I had built was firmly anchored in the people strategy; the opportunity was to get more embedded into the business strategy. The African American resource group saw the opportunity as well and wanted to change that. Rather than encouraging the company to give a donation or issue a statement, they wanted to make an impact and contribute on the product side, something that had never been done before.

The data supported their instinct. Marketing research showed that women of color, specifically African American and Latina women, stayed in stores longest and spent the most per visit. Yet the product development process had not yet created any products that were targeted specifically to them.

Armed with this data, my team and ERG representatives proposed creating product collections aligned with heritage months. February would feature a Black History Month collection. March would honor Women's History Month. The calendar would continue through Pride Month and beyond, and a percentage of the proceeds of the collections would go to nonprofit organizations that the company already had partnered with, deepening the relationships across communities they were invested in.

Getting buy-in required persistence. The team's initial response reflected years of operating in a particular way:

"Those are nice ideas, but we know what we're doing. We have a very specific brand point of view." There was real protectiveness around the creative process; a belief that outside perspectives might dilute rather than enhance the brand.

This is a moment when real inclusive leadership was needed, and we found that in Paula. Paula was a senior marketing VP willing to try something different. Her openness to change made everything possible.

What followed was collaboration in action. Paula connected the ERG leaders with the right marketing teams. We conducted focus groups with real customers, bringing in women of color to react to product names, packaging designs, and scent profiles. Employees who had never been part of product development sat in those sessions, hearing directly from customers about what resonated and what fell flat.

The feedback was invaluable. Customers responded to themes of empowerment and visibility. They wanted to see themselves reflected in the products they purchased. They appreciated when a brand acknowledged their cultural significance rather than treating them as an afterthought. There's power in being seen.

The ERG packaged this feedback and worked with Paula and the marketing and design teams to create a Black History Month capsule collection. The collection represented months of cross-functional partnership, bringing together perspectives that had never collaborated before. So much pride and joy and expectation of success.

The collection launched. And then everything fell apart.

By the time the products reached stores, I had left the company for another opportunity. This time, I wasn't leaving because of something I wanted to get away from; this time I was going toward something greater. Ironically, Paula ended up taking a leave of absence, so this effort was without its primary champions.

Without my team's continued involvement and the support of marketing leadership, the partnership that had created the collection was not maintained throughout the product lifecycle. The marketing team, reverting to old habits, decided they knew how to make the displays look appealing without further input from the ERGs.

They ended up making one of those cultural faux pas that make people ask, "What were they thinking?"

If anyone from the ERGs had been consulted, they would have immediately flagged the problem. The images went viral. Social media erupted with disbelief. I learned that the company pulled the collection and cancelled the other heritage month capsules that had been planned.

I tell this story not as a failure, but as a lesson about what is possible when leaders create space for new possibilities, what happens in a leadership vacuum, and what true partnership requires. The creation of that collection demonstrated the power of collaboration across difference. Employees with cultural knowledge worked alongside marketing professionals with product expertise.

And it all took place in the space that Paula created. Together, the marketing, DEI, and ERG teams created something neither group could have developed alone. This is what "leading from the front" looks like.

But collaboration is not a one-time event. It requires sustained commitment through every phase of execution. When the partnership ended prematurely, the cultural blindness that the ERG had been brought in to address reasserted itself with predictable results.

The skeptics who had resisted the collaboration from the beginning said, "I told you so." But those of us who had been part of the process knew the truth. The failure was not proof that collaboration does not work. It was proof that collaboration cannot be abandoned halfway through.

What Lasted

Despite that painful ending, seeds planted during that period continued to grow.

The environmental ERG had been advocating for more sustainable product materials. At the time, their proposals were dismissed with the same rationale: "That is not our brand. Our customers come for the sense of discovery."

Years later, those stores now feature many sustainable products. They expanded into different product lines, ideas that were summarily dismissed when first proposed. I see more and more brands designing products without gender-specific marketing, developing adaptive clothing, incorporating inclusive design that welcomes all customers rather than targeting what was once considered to be a "standard" demographic.

My team had also redesigned the name tags worn by store employees, adding insignia for which ERGs they belonged to. We created a customer manifesto, a visible sign in every store declaring that everyone was welcome. We developed learning courses on engaging customers across difference and worked with loss prevention on culturally aware de-escalation techniques.

Even though I no longer work there, I still shop there regularly. The signs remain. The name tags still feature those inclusive elements. The diversity among store employees is visible. The core elements of what we developed continues to shape how they engage customers and employees.

That is the legacy of this work, even when individual "initiatives" end painfully. What you build—into infrastructure, into learning and development, into culture —outlasts any single project's success or failure. And we will dig into that even more in the following chapter.

You have learned to lead from the DJ booth. To create conditions where authentic expression can flourish. To guide without controlling. To build energy without forcing it.

But the DJ booth is just one room in the house. In the next chapter, we will look at the infrastructure level, where the pipes and wires run. We will learn how to design systems that connect rather than separate, that naturally produce fair outcomes without requiring superhuman effort from individuals.

Chapter 5
Good Life
The Infrastructure

Once you get that good life feeling, let me tell you
no one can take it away.

— Inner City, "Good Life"

That line is not just optimism. It is a design principle.

*Feelings fade. Leaders move on. Programs get cut. If
belonging depends on the right people being in the right
mood, it will not survive the next reorganization.*

*But infrastructure persists. The policies that determine
who gets hired, who gets promoted, whose voice gets heard
—these systems keep running whether anyone is paying
attention or not. And they produce outcomes, fair or unfair,
long after the people who designed them have moved on.*

*This chapter is about building infrastructure that makes
the good life possible for everyone. Through systems*

designed so well that equity becomes the default. When the pipes work for all, no one can take that away.

You cannot love your way to equity if the infrastructure is broken.

When the Mix Makes All the Difference

I was three months into my new role as Chief Diversity Officer at a company when I discovered something that would change how I thought about creating fair systems forever. We had just completed our annual employee satisfaction survey, and the results were puzzling. Overall, people loved working there. But when we broke down the data by demographics, a troubling pattern emerged.

Women and people of color had significantly lower scores on questions about career advancement opportunities and feeling valued for their contributions. At first, we assumed it was about individual managers or specific team dynamics. But as I dug deeper, talking to employees and analyzing our processes, I realized something more fundamental was happening.

Our promotion system looked fair on paper. Everyone had the same performance review process, the same advancement criteria, the same development opportunities. But that same treatment was producing very different outcomes for different people. It was like a building where the water pressure is strong on the first floor but barely a trickle by the time it reaches the top. Same pipes. Same system. Very different experience depending on where you stand.

The problem was not bad people making biased decisions. The problem was that our systems had been designed by and for a specific group of people, and they carried forward assumptions about what normal career paths, communication styles, and success looked like.

That is when I understood that creating inclusive communities is not just about changing hearts and minds. It is about designing systems that naturally produce good outcomes for everyone, just like Inner City sang about everyone having a right to the good life.

When the Stated System Is Not the Real System

I learned this lesson early in my career, before I had the language of infrastructure to describe what I was seeing.

My first job in DEI was as a diversity recruiter at a professional services firm. I was responsible for building the pipeline of diverse talent across skill areas. I was filling in for another recruiter who was on leave when an accounting position came open. I was told this would be a lay-up to fill, since there was already a contractor on the team who applied for the job, a Black woman who had been doing the work for months. She knew the systems, understood the business, had relationships with the stakeholders. When I reviewed her resume and conducted my interview, she met every requirement in the job description. Not most of them. Every single one.

I also interviewed a white male candidate who came through an employee referral. Solid experience, but he did not have the years the role required. He had not supported this part of the business. He was missing technical skills outlined in the description.

Both candidates interviewed with me and the hiring manager. The hiring manager wanted to extend the offer to the white male candidate.

I asked him to help me understand.

"He really had the personality," the manager explained. "Seemed to be a great fit with the team. He doesn't have all the specific things, but he struck me as very ambitious and a fast learner."

I pressed further. What about the other candidate? She was already there. Already doing a good job.

"She's fine in a technical capacity," he said. "But from a full-time perspective, we need someone who can be more strategic. Who's good at building relationships."

There it was. The stated system, the job description, the requirements, the criteria he had given me, was not the real system. The real system was operating on a different set of criteria entirely: personality, fit, potential, ambition. Words that meant one thing when applied to one candidate and something else when applied to another.

This is what broken infrastructure looks like. Not malice. Not intentional discrimination. A hiring process that allowed subjective criteria to override stated requirements without anyone noticing the switch. A system designed to be objective but that produced subjective outcomes because no guardrails existed to prevent it.

I asked if I could have a coaching conversation with the hiring manager about what I was observing. My manager said that was okay, but ultimately the decision was his.

So, I scheduled the time. I framed it carefully: the criteria he had outlined did not match who he wanted to hire. The candidate already on his team met all the stated requirements. The candidate he preferred did not. How should I think about serving my clients when what is stated is not what gets selected?

He got defensive immediately. "What are you saying? I'm a manager. I should be able to hire who I want to hire."

He hired who he wanted to hire. The Black woman who had been doing the job continued as a contractor for a while longer. Then she moved on.

The outcome was not pretty. But the lesson stayed with me: infrastructure that looks neutral can still produce biased outcomes if it allows unstated criteria to override stated ones. The job description was a pipe that looked like it carried water to everyone equally. But somewhere between the description and the decision, the pressure changed. The candidate who matched what was written got a trickle. The candidate who matched what was unwritten got the flow.

Fixing this requires more than good intentions. It requires redesigning the infrastructure itself, building in checkpoints where decisions must be validated against stated criteria, creating accountability for when they diverge, making the invisible visible before it becomes a pattern.

That hiring manager probably did not think of himself as biased. He thought he was exercising good judgment. But the system gave him permission to substitute his comfort over the business need as outlined in the job requirements, and no one had built in a mechanism to catch it.

When Advancement Becomes a Barrier

The recruiter story showed how broken infrastructure affects who gets hired. But the pipes carry water through the entire building, not just the entrance. The same design flaws that produce unequal outcomes in hiring can produce unequal outcomes at every stage of the employee lifecycle, including the moment that's supposed to be a reward.

Angela was a powerhouse. District managers requested visits to her store specifically to observe how she operated. Her customer engagement scores were exceptional. Her sales numbers consistently topped the region. She was exactly the kind of talent organizations say they want to develop and advance.

So, when she was offered a promotion to a multi-store management role, everyone expected her to be thrilled.

Instead, she faced an impossible choice.

The promotion came with increased base pay and expanded responsibility. On paper, it looked like recognition of her outstanding performance. But Angela had done the math, and the math did not work.

As a top-performing salesperson, Angela earned significant bonuses for meeting and exceeding her targets. These "kickers" had become a substantial part of her total income. She had structured her family's finances around that predictable compensation.

The management role eliminated access to those performance bonuses. Yes, her base salary would increase. But her actual take-home pay would decrease, potentially by thousands of dollars annually.

There was also the matter of her schedule. Angela was caring for both her children and her aging parents. Her current role offered predictability. She knew her hours. She could arrange childcare and eldercare around a consistent schedule. The multi-store position would require travel between locations, unpredictable hours, and flexibility she simply did not have.

When Angela expressed hesitation about the promotion, the response from leadership revealed a fundamental weakness in how the organization thought about advancement.

They perceived her as ungrateful.

The assumption was that everyone wants to be promoted, that upward mobility is universally desirable, that anyone who hesitates must not appreciate the opportunity being offered. No one paused to ask what barriers might make this "opportunity" feel like a burden.

When I learned about Angela's situation, I saw it as a systems problem, not a performance problem or an attitude problem. The promotion structure had been designed by people who did not need to worry about losing bonus income or arranging care for multiple generations of family members. The system was not intentionally exclusionary. It simply never accounted for circumstances different from those of the people who designed it.

I worked with HR and the stores leadership team to approach this differently.

First, we had to help them see Angela's actual situation, rather than their assumptions about it. This was not about being ungrateful. This was about a talented employee facing real financial and logistical constraints that made a standard promotion package unworkable.

Second, we had to think about equity rather than equality. Giving Angela the exact same promotion package as everyone else would produce an unequal outcome because she was not starting from the same circumstances. True equity meant ensuring she got what she needed to be successful, even if that looked different from the standard template.

We explored the full range of possibilities. Could we restructure her schedule to accommodate her caregiving responsibilities? Could we offer a signing bonus or transition payment to offset the loss of performance kickers during her first year? Could we look at the total rewards package, including benefits, flexibility, and professional development, rather than focusing solely on base salary?

The conversations took time. They required people to think creatively about a situation they had never encountered, or more accurately, had never noticed before. How many other high performers had quietly declined promotions or left the company entirely because the advancement pathway did not work for their circumstances?

Eventually, a package was assembled that addressed Angela's actual needs. Her schedule was structured in partnership with her district manager to accommodate her family obligations. Financial components were adjusted to ensure she was not taking a pay cut to accept more responsibility.

Angela stepped into the role and succeeded.

But the larger lesson was not about one employee. It was about how systems that appear neutral can systematically disadvantage people whose lives do not match the assumptions of the system designers.

The promotion structure was not designed with malicious intent. It was designed by people who had never needed to count on bonus income to make ends meet, who had never been the primary caregiver for both children and aging parents, who had never had to calculate whether career advancement was financially feasible.

When we design systems, we embed our assumptions into them. If we want those systems to work for everyone, we have to actively seek out the perspectives of people whose circumstances differ from our own. We have to ask who this system might not work for and then redesign accordingly.

Angela's story had a happy ending because someone surfaced the problem and leadership was willing to think creatively about solutions. But how many Angelas never speak up? How many simply decline the promotion, or leave for a competitor, or never apply in the first place because they have already calculated that advancement is not designed for people like them?

That is the hidden cost of systems that only work for some people. You never see the talent you are losing because the loss is invisible. The Angelas of the world do not complain. They just quietly opt out of pathways that were never built for them.

What the Pipes Teach Us

Two stories. Two different failure points. The same underlying problem.

In the first, a hiring manager's unstated preferences overrode the stated job requirements. In the second, an advancement system designed for one type of life punished anyone living differently. Neither system was built with malicious intent. Both produced outcomes that contradicted the organization's stated values.

This is what it means to examine infrastructure. Not hunting for villains, but tracing outcomes back to the design choices that produced them. Asking who was in the room when this system was created, and who was not. Asking whose circumstances were treated as default, and whose were never considered.

The work is not dramatic. It is methodical. You study how systems actually function, not how they are supposed to function. You listen to the people experiencing different outcomes and let their expertise guide the redesign. You test changes and measure whether they produce the equity you intended. You build in accountability so the fixes survive the next leadership transition.

And you accept that this work is never finished. Systems drift. Contexts change. New populations arrive with circumstances no one anticipated. The pipes need ongoing maintenance, not a one-time repair.

But when the infrastructure works, when the water pressure reaches every floor, something remarkable happens. You stop having to compensate for broken systems with heroic individual effort. Equity becomes the default rather than the exception. The good life Inner City sang about becomes structurally possible for everyone, not just those lucky enough to have managers who fight for them.

That is what we are building toward. Not perfect systems; those do not exist. But systems that work for more people, more of the time, with less effort required to overcome them.

You cannot love your way to equity if the infrastructure is broken. But you can rebuild the pipes.

Chapter 6
Feel The Drive
The Foundation

You must feel the drive, get into the stride.

— Doctor's Cat, "Feel the Drive"

Every building needs a foundation. Something solid to stand on. Something that connects the structure to the ground beneath it.

The foundation of the World House is history. Not history as a burden, but history as bedrock. Understanding where we come from, what has been built before, what has been destroyed, and what we owe to those who laid the groundwork.

This chapter is about learning to build on that foundation. To honor what came before while creating something new. To feel the drive that connects past to present to future.

The Foundations That Formed Me

The three-flat on Ingleside Avenue in Chicago's Chatham neighborhood was my first World House. We lived on the top floor—and that long walk up every day was a beast.

My grandparents raised me because my mother was a single parent working nights. But their place was not just home to me. My grandmother, Minnie Hudson—everyone called her Mama—and my grandfather William—who we all called Uncle Bill because Mama did not initially want her kids to know she was dating another man after their father left, and the name stuck even after they married— were foster parents to more than twenty children over the years. They adopted four and raised four of their own, plus me and my cousin Will. Anywhere from four to eight kids in the house at any given time. Sometimes more.

Children came from different circumstances, different family situations, different starting points. Some stayed for years. Some stayed for months. All of them were treated as family from the moment they walked through the door. Most of my childhood was spent with my adopted aunts and uncles Tawanda (Tee), Lindell (Linn) and Caroline. Because it was too much to explain my unique family situation, and we were close in age, they became my brothers and sisters and remain so to this day.

The four of us couldn't have been more different. Tee was fierce and mischievous, super smart and always getting into something. Linn was laid back but silly—he could always make us laugh. Caroline was a firecracker who lived by her own rules. And then me: the quiet, nerdy kid who always had her ear by a speaker, hands writing stories, or nose in a book.

While we each brought our unique challenges, Mama did not distinguish between her adopted children, her foster children, or her grandchildren. The household ran on simple principles: Everyone is family, everyone contributes, everyone is held to the same expectations of respect and responsibility. And her word was the law!

Those principles did not come from nowhere. They came from what Mama and Uncle Bill had survived.

Mama grew up as Minnie on a sharecropper's farm in Clark County, Arkansas, during the time of Jim Crow laws. She rarely shared details—I imagine the memories were too heavy to revisit casually—but sometimes, when she was schooling me on something important, the history would surface. The back-breaking work. The poverty. The daily indignities designed to remind Black people that they were less than human. And then the courage it took to pack up and move north with a sixth-grade education and a few dollars to her name, carrying a hope that Chicago might offer something better.

Uncle Bill had his own scars from home and abroad. He was raised in Texarkana, Texas, a city with a brutal history of racial violence against Black people. He was also a World War II veteran who survived the Battle of the Bulge. But what I remember most is not the pain he carried. It is what he did with it.

By the time I was born, he was retired but served as a poll worker and election judge. Every election day, he would come home with stories about helping our community exercise its most fundamental right. Democracy was not abstract to him. It was a right he had fought for on the battlefield. It was neighbors showing up at the church basement or the school gym, casting their votes, making their voices count. He had fought in the ugliest of wars, defending democracy overseas while Black people at home were beaten and killed for trying to exercise it. Now he spent his retirement making sure every single person in our precinct could cast their vote.

Mama was a no-nonsense but loving matriarch who watched the news almost religiously. I would sit right beside her as she yelled at the television about local politics, especially during Harold Washington's time as mayor, when the "Council Wars" were in full effect. White aldermen were openly blocking the city's first Black mayor at every turn, and Mama took it personally. In my young brain, I was trying to decipher what was happening so I could have informed conversations with her about the latest shenanigans. She was teaching me that staying informed was not optional—it was a responsibility. The world was not going to fix itself. You had to pay attention. You had to show up.

Uncle Bill was the kindest person I have ever known, soft-spoken and genteel but with sharp looks when he meant business. Even as an adult, he would hold my hand when we crossed the street. There was a tenderness in him that felt almost radical—a Black man in America who had refused to let the violence of his era harden his heart.

Both of them lived by the principle that to whom much is given, much is required.

One evening, as we watched Harold Washington on the news, I made a comment that came across as if I didn't care that he was Black. Mama turned to me and said something I have never forgotten.

> *Girl, you need to know where you come from, so you know where you are going. This freedom you have, this education, these opportunities—they did not just appear out of nowhere. They were paid for with somebody else's blood, sweat, and tears.*

She was not telling me this to make me feel guilty. She was not trying to burden me with anger or resentment. She was laying a foundation. Helping me understand that I was not the first builder; I was a link in a lineage. That honoring the past meant using its lessons to build a future where other children would not have to face what she had faced.

Decades later, I would understand just how much courage that journey required.

In January 2024, I spent a day at the Legacy Museum and memorial sites in Montgomery, Alabama, with a group of DEI leaders, hosted by the founder, Bryan Stevenson. The exhibits were breathtaking and painful—the history of lynching and racial violence against Black Americans laid bare in its most undeniable truth. Seeing it together, in that space, with people who had dedicated their careers to justice, changed something in all of us.

Bryan facilitated several conversations throughout the day, reminding us that we were the torch bearers of justice in American institutions. That witnessing the horrors of the past was not meant to break us. It was meant to ensure that we would fight to protect the liberties that were purchased with so much suffering. That we would be the change we wished to see in the world.

But the most personal moment came at the National Monument to Freedom.

The monument is massive, a soaring, expansive wall of stone etched with more than 100,000 chosen family surnames, an exercise of newfound liberty that the formerly enslaved could choose after the Emancipation Proclamation. These names represented freedom, independence, and hope for the future as millions fled in the Great Migration from the South to the North and West. This monument forged a connection to the courage, strength, and resilience of our ancestors that we could reach out and touch. The names were not listed alphabetically. They are arranged by frequency in the archival records.

I looked for my grandparents' surnames. Hudson. Carr. I expected them to be in completely different places on the wall. Different letters, different frequencies, no reason to be anywhere near each other.

But there they were. Side by side. Etched in stone. Right next to each other.

I broke open. The kind of crying that takes over your whole body, as if time collapses and the people you love step back into the room. For a moment, it felt like they were there with me, close enough to touch, close enough to hug just one more time.

What are the odds? Out of a hundred thousand surnames, arranged not by alphabet but by frequency, my grandmother's family name and my grandfather's family name had landed together—as if the wall itself knew they would find each other, as if the monument had already written their love story into the record.

I found Bryan and showed him. I could barely get the words out. He has immortalized my grandparents together, I told him. I cried on his shoulder. He brought some of his team over and eventually shared my story with the entire group.

"This is why I created this monument," he said. "Nowhere else in this country can Black Americans pay tribute to their own families who did something so brave—and made the lives we are living today possible."

Mama had told me to know where I came from. Bryan Stevenson built a wall that showed me.

I did not fully understand until years later what my grandparents had given me. Not just a place to live, but a model. A working example of what it looks like to build community across difference, to welcome people whose circumstances are not your own, to create belonging through daily practice rather than grand gestures.

When I walked into my first corporate role and started thinking about how to create inclusive cultures, I was not starting from theory. I was starting from Mama's plastic-covered sofa where kids from everywhere became family. I was starting from Uncle Bill's quiet insistence that everyone deserves dignity and a voice. I was starting from a three-flat on Ingleside that held more dedication than most mansions ever will.

The foundation was already laid. I just had to recognize what I was standing on.

The Foundation Beneath the Beat

While I was learning to build community in that three-flat on Ingleside, another foundation was being laid across the city, one I would inherit a few years later when my cousin Will took me to that gymnasium at Mendel.

In the Introduction, I told you about my discovery: how a late-night workshop design session in a hotel room connected the death of disco to the birth of House music, and how that connection unlocked everything I understood about this work. But I have not yet told you the full origin story—the lineage that made that gymnasium possible.

It started with a group of young Black gay friends in 1974 who wanted to experience the disco scene sweeping the nation. Chicago's premiere gay discotheque was not welcoming to them, so they traveled to New York to experience the legendary loft parties there. They fell in love with the freedom, the energy, the openness. But they could not keep making that trip. So one of their mothers asked a simple question:

"Why can't y'all just have parties here?"

That question changed music history.

They started throwing parties in apartments, then warehouses, building a following through word of mouth and handmade flyers. In 1977, they opened a club at 206 South Jefferson with a young DJ from New York named Frankie Knuckles. People started asking each other:

"You going to the Warehouse?"

The rest, as they say, is history.

You already know what came next, how disco was declared dead at Comiskey Park in 1979, how the communities who created it refused to disappear, how they went underground and transformed rejection into innovation. What I want you to understand now is what they built in those underground spaces. Not just a sound, but a philosophy.

As Professor Fredara Hadley of the Juilliard School observes in the WTTW documentary *House Music: A Cultural Revolution*: "America loves the music of Black people, but not always the actual Black people who create it."[1]

---

1. Gail Baker, *House Music: A Cultural Revolution, WTTW, 2024.*

The Warehouse and the clubs that followed were a direct response to that truth. They created something radical for their time: spaces where marginalized people could gather safely and be fully themselves. Black, Brown, gay, straight —it did not matter once you stepped onto that floor. The music either moved you or it did not. The only credential required was your willingness to surrender to the rhythm.

Professor Hadley captures the principle that made these spaces revolutionary: "If queer Black people are safe, then everybody else is going to be safe."

That idea, that safety flows outward from the most vulnerable, became the foundation of House culture. And it is the same principle that guides my inclusion work today. When you design for the margins, the center benefits, too. When you create conditions where the most excluded can thrive, everyone thrives.

Something happened on those dance floors that went beyond entertainment. People who had been rejected everywhere else found acceptance. People who had to hide their identities all week could be fully themselves for one night. The music became church for people who had been told they were not welcome in traditional sanctuaries. The dancing became prayer.

I think about the bedroom producers, like me, creating entire genres with nothing but a drum machine and a Casio keyboard. I spent hours in my room splicing cassette tapes and creating tracks on my keyboard, trying to emulate The Hot Mix 5. I think about the women DJs who were told they did not have the coordination to mix, who wore baggy sweatshirts and baseball caps to hide their gender until they had already proven themselves with the music. I think about the high school parties that kept Catholic schools open on the South Side, introducing a whole generation to sounds they would carry for the rest of their lives.

I think about Frankie Knuckles, who became the Godfather of House, who won a Grammy, who got a street named after him, who collaborated with everyone from Michael Jackson to Beyoncé. Near the end of his life, he said something about Chicago that speaks a truth about the city that shaped my worldview:

> *People make eye contact with you, and when they do, they say hello. Nowhere else in the world do you get it the way you get it here. It says a lot because it makes you feel like you belong.*

He passed away in 2014, but what he built did not die with him. The Warehouse is now an official Chicago landmark. The Chosen Few still throw their festival every July. A new generation of DJs and producers is carrying the sound forward, bold, audacious, creating space without waiting for permission.

That is what it means to inherit a foundation. Not just to stand on what others built, but to keep building. To honor the lineage by extending it. To create space for people who will come after you, the same way space was created for you.

The three-flat on Ingleside taught me that community is daily practice. The dance floors of Chicago taught me that belonging can scale, from a living room to a warehouse to a festival of tens of thousands to the world. Both foundations hold me up. Both remind me that I am not the first builder, and I will not be the last.

The only question is what I will add before I pass the tools to the next generation.

Chapter 7
The Music Sounds Better with You
The Dance Floor

I feel like the music sounds better with you.

> — Stardust, "Music Sounds Better
> with You"

This is the room you have been working toward. The dance floor. The space where everyone can move together while maintaining what makes them unique.

All the demolition, the blueprints, the mobilization, the leadership, the infrastructure, the foundation—it all leads here. To a room where belonging is not just possible but inevitable. Where the music truly does sound better with everyone.

This chapter is about creating that room. Helping people belong. Designing for differences. Making sure the music changes once people arrive.

When the Music Failed Someone

It was 1998, and Stardust's "Music Sounds Better with You" became an instant classic that captured something universal: Everything is better when we are together. But here is what made that track special. It was not just about adding more people to the mix. It was about how different elements—the guitar sample, the vocals, the beat—each maintained their unique qualities while creating something none of them could have achieved alone.

I experienced the opposite of that magic before. At one company, we had worked so hard to get it right. Our work-force was diverse. Our policies were progressive. Our learning and development programs were comprehensive. On paper, we had built a dance floor and filled it with talented people from every background.

But someone asked to speak with me on her way out the door, and what she told me shattered the illusion that presence equals belonging.

The Exit Interview that Changed Everything

She asked for the meeting. That was unusual. Most departing employees complete their exit interviews as a formality, offering polite generalities about pursuing new opportunities, thanking the team, wishing everyone well. This engineer wanted to be heard.

She was a Black woman in a technical role at a company where women in engineering were already rare, and Black women were rarer still. She had navigated being the only, or one of the few, throughout her education at an elite engineering program and across her professional career. That experience alone was not what drove her out.

What broke her was the constant, quiet erosion of her sense of self.

She described a culture where her credentials were perpetually questioned. Colleagues assumed she had been admitted through some "special program" rather than on her own merit. When other engineers made mistakes, they corrected them and moved on. When she made a single error, it was called out in meetings. Her competence was treated as perpetually provisional, always requiring re-proof.

She had discovered she was being paid less than peers in identical roles. This was before we implemented standardized pay structures, when compensation was negotiated individually. And the research is clear: men ask for more, while women, particularly women of color, tend to accept initial offers or request less. The system was not rigged by any single person's malice. It was rigged by its own design.

She described feeling like she was running up a down escalator. No matter how hard she worked, the treadmill moved faster.

But the most painful part was what happened when she sought help. She reported her experiences to HR and to her manager. The response, every time, focused on what *she* could do differently. Maybe she should find ways to build better relationships with her teammates. Maybe she should focus on her work to avoid errors. The system that was supposed to support her instead suggested the problem was hers to solve.

She did not feel heard. She did not feel valued. She did not feel like she belonged. So, she left.

I sat with her experience long after that conversation ended. She was what we call a regrettable loss, one where their absence would have a significant impact on performance, production, and team morale. Here was a talented engineer from an elite program, exactly the kind of technical talent that technology companies compete fiercely to attract, walking out the door because the culture had made her feel worthless.

We had invited her to the party. We had not changed the music.

What One Voice Revealed About the Whole Room

Her story was not isolated. As we dug deeper, we found patterns. Women in technical roles across demographic categories were reporting similar experiences. The specific manifestations varied: some felt excluded from decision-making, others felt their ideas were only valued when repeated by someone else, others described an exhausting performance of fitting in that left no energy for actual performance. But the underlying dynamic was consistent. A culture that worked well for some people was systematically undermining others.

This is the gap between inclusion and belonging. Inclusion is who is in the room. Belonging is whether the room changes to welcome them. We had achieved the first without ever attempting the second.

The exit interview forced me to confront a hard truth: You can have every program, every policy, every stated commitment to diversity, and still lose the people you most need to keep because belonging is not built with programs. It is built with the daily experience of being seen, valued, and supported in ways that match who you actually are, not who the system assumes you should be.

I had been measuring diversity and teaching inclusion. I needed to start designing for belonging.

The Redesign

Her exit interview became a catalyst for systemic change.

We launched what we called an HR transformation, a comprehensive redesign of the structures that shaped employee experience. Not a new training program. Not a town hall about values. A fundamental reconstruction of the systems that determined how people were hired, paid, evaluated, supported, and advanced.

We created standardized job families with clear levels and transparent criteria for advancement. We established pay ranges tied to those levels so that compensation was determined by role and experience rather than negotiation skill or previous salary history.

The pay equity implications were immediate. When you standardize ranges, you eliminate the compounding disadvantage that follows employees from job to job. A woman who was underpaid at her previous company would no longer carry that penalty into her new role. The range for the position was the range, regardless of what someone earned before.

We addressed the feedback and support systems that had failed this engineer. HR's role should be to champion employees, not to reflexively defend managers or redirect complaints back onto the people raising them. We trained HR partners to recognize patterns of exclusion and to intervene in the systems producing those patterns rather than coaching individuals to tolerate them.

We redesigned how teams operated. Meeting agendas were adjusted to include written components where people could contribute asynchronously. Brainstorming sessions built in reflection time before discussion. Multiple channels existed for sharing ideas, not just whoever spoke fastest in the room. We looked at how performance was evaluated and made sure the criteria reflected actual contribution, not just the kind of contribution that was most visible to people who already held power.

None of this happened overnight. Structural change requires sustained attention, resources, and willingness to examine practices that feel normal precisely because they have always been done that way.

But every change followed the same principle: instead of asking people to adapt to a culture that was not designed for them, we redesigned the culture to bring out the best in everyone.

The Engineer Who Stayed

Not every story ends in departure. Let me tell you about someone whose different style was overlooked until the culture shifted.

We had a brilliant engineer who never spoke up in meetings. The engineering culture at the time valued quick verbal processing: the ability to think out loud, to jump into rapid-fire technical debates, to advocate loudly for your ideas. This was what "engagement" looked like, and leaders rewarded it accordingly.

This engineer processed differently. She needed time to think before speaking. By the time she had formulated her response, the conversation had moved on. Her manager interpreted her silence as disengagement or lack of ideas.

After we began redesigning how teams operated—adding written brainstorming, building in reflection time, and creating multiple pathways for contribution—her experience changed completely.

The engineer who had been overlooked emerged as one of the most thoughtful technical contributors on her team. Her analyses were more thorough because she took time with them. Her solutions were more creative because she considered angles that rapid-fire debate missed. She had not changed. The system had changed to recognize her style of contribution.

She stayed and thrived. She became an advocate for creating space for different working styles because she had experienced firsthand the difference it made.

Two engineers. Same company. Same technical excellence. One left because the culture could not see her. One stayed because the culture learned to.

That is the difference between a dance floor where everyone is expected to move the same way and a dance floor where every style of movement makes the music better.

The HARMONY Framework: Designing the Dance Floor

Those two stories, the engineer who left and the engineer who stayed, taught me that belonging is not a feeling you can mandate. It is an outcome you design for. The systems, the structures, the daily practices of how people interact: these either produce belonging or they do not. And hoping for it without designing for it is how you lose your best people while congratulating yourself on your diversity numbers.

Over years of practice across multiple organizations, I developed a framework for creating environments where belonging is the default rather than the exception. I call it HARMONY, because like the musical concept it is named for, it is about distinct voices contributing to something richer than any single voice could create alone.

H: Honor Different Styles

The engineer who stayed illustrated this principle more clearly than any research paper could. She was brilliant. Her manager thought she was disengaged. The gap between those two realities was not a people problem—it was a design problem.

Honoring different styles means building environments that accommodate multiple ways of being, communicating, and contributing—not as special accommodations, but as standard operating procedure.

In practice, this meant redesigning meetings to include both verbal and written participation. It meant creating asynchronous channels where people could contribute ideas on their own timeline. It meant coaching managers to recognize that silence is not absence; it might be the deepest form of thinking in the room.

The engineer who left had a different style, too. She described colleagues who questioned her credentials or who treated her competence as provisional. That is what happens when a culture has an unspoken template for what a "real engineer" looks and sounds like, and anyone who deviates from that template has to prove themselves over and over again.

Honoring different styles is not about lowering standards. It is about recognizing that excellence has more than one expression.

In practice: Notice how different people in your environment prefer to communicate and contribute. Create multiple pathways for participation. Evaluate people on the quality of their thinking, not on how closely their style matches the dominant culture's expectations.

A: Appreciate Unique Contributions

The engineer's exit interview story is a case study in what happens when unique contributions go unappreciated. She had the credentials. She had the skills. But the culture only recognized contribution when it came in a particular package—the package of someone who looked, sounded, and socialized like the people who had always been there.

Appreciation is not a compliment in a meeting. It is a system that recognizes and rewards different forms of value creation. At this same company, we redesigned our recognition and advancement criteria to capture contributions that had been invisible before: mentoring junior engineers, translating complex technical concepts for non-technical stakeholders, identifying risks that others missed because they were moving too fast.

One of the most powerful changes was this: We stopped treating "culture fit" as a hiring criterion and started asking about "culture add." Instead of "Will this person fit in with who we already are?" we asked "What will this person bring that we do not already have?" That single reframe changed who got hired, who was valued, and what the organization was capable of producing.

In practice: Audit who gets recognized and for what. Ask whether your systems reward one type of contribution while ignoring others that are equally valuable. Design recognition to be as diverse as the people you want to retain.

R: Rotate Power and Decision-Making

In the chapters on infrastructure and leadership, I shared stories about what happens when the same people always control the decisions, how unstated criteria override stated ones, and how assumptions become invisible because the people making decisions all share the same assumptions.

Rotating power means ensuring that people from different backgrounds have real influence over decisions that affect them. Not advisory roles. Not suggestion boxes. Actual authority.

Think back to the story about Paula and the employee resource group product ideas. ERGs had been advisory only: They could raise concerns, but the decision-makers were free to ignore them. When we gave them budget authority, seats at the product development table, and accountability for outcomes, the results were transformative. Products reached customers who had never been considered before. Revenue grew in markets that had been written off. Innovation accelerated because the range of perspectives informing decisions expanded dramatically.

The exit interview engineer had reported her concerns to HR and her manager. Both redirected the problem back to her. That is what happens when the people with power to change systems never have to experience the systems they have built. Rotating power means the people affected by a decision have a voice in making it.

In practice: Look at who makes decisions in your environment. If the same demographic profile consistently holds power, create structures that rotate leadership, share authority, and require input from people whose experience differs from the decision-makers.

M: Make Space for Authentic Relationships

The exit interview engineer described a culture where she had to perform a version of herself to make other people comfortable. Every interaction required calculation: what to share, what to hide, how to present herself in ways that would not trigger the assumptions she knew her colleagues carried.

That performance is exhausting. And it is the enemy of belonging.

Making space for authentic relationships means creating conditions where people can be known as whole human beings, not just as job titles or demographic categories. It means building interpersonal connections that go beyond the transactional.

Across multiple companies, I've seen that some of the most effective belonging strategies were surprisingly simple: Cross-functional projects where people worked together on problems outside their usual scope. Mentoring circles that connected people across levels and departments. Team rituals that made space for personal sharing—not forced vulnerability, but organic opportunities to learn about each other's lives, interests, and perspectives.

The engineer who stayed described a moment after the redesign when her manager asked about her weekend. That particular weekend was significant since she attended her cousin's wedding ceremony and festivities. The engineer, who is of Indian descent, talked about the traditions and the celebrations and found that her manager was fully engaged with her experience and even asked to see pictures. It sounds small. How meaningful is a casual conversation about the weekend? But it was not small. It was the first time she felt like a person at work rather than a function.

In practice: Create opportunities for people to connect beyond their roles. Design social interactions that appeal to different cultural and personal preferences, not just happy hours. Encourage leaders to know their people as humans, not just as employees.

O: Organize Around Shared Purpose

On a House music dance floor, thousands of people with nothing in common can move together for hours. The music gives them a shared purpose that transcends every difference.

In organizations, shared purpose works the same way. When people understand how their unique contributions connect to something larger, something they all care about, differences become assets rather than obstacles.

After the exit interview, one of the most powerful changes we made was connecting our redesign work explicitly to the company's mission. This was not about being nice to diverse employees or another HR initiative that becomes a distraction to the business. This was about building a company capable of producing its best work. When engineers from different backgrounds contribute their best thinking, the products improve. When pay equity attracts and retains top talent, the company outperforms competitors. When teams operate inclusively, innovation accelerates.

Framing belonging as a business imperative, not just a moral one, gave everyone a reason to invest in the work, including the skeptics.

In practice: Regularly connect individual contributions to organizational mission. Help people see how different perspectives improve outcomes. Build shared goals that everyone can rally around while contributing in their own way.

N: Nurture Growth for Everyone

In Chapter 5, we met Angela, the top-performing store manager whose promotion would have been a pay cut because the advancement system was designed for someone with a different life. Her story revealed how systems that appear neutral can systematically disadvantage people whose circumstances differ from the designers' assumptions.

Nurturing growth means creating development pathways that work with people's strengths and circumstances rather than demanding that everyone follow the same trajectory. Not everyone defines advancement the same way. Not everyone can access development opportunities offered at the same time, in the same format, through the same channels.

At the tech company, this meant offering development in multiple formats, not just in-person workshops during business hours. It meant creating technical and management tracks so engineers did not have to abandon their craft to advance. It meant supporting lateral moves as legitimate career development, not just upward ones.

The exit interview engineer had been on a treadmill, running harder to reach a finish line that kept moving. Growth for her was not about more training. It was about a system that recognized her trajectory rather than forcing her into someone else's.

In practice: Audit your development and advancement pathways. Ask who they work for and who they do not. Create multiple routes to growth that accommodate different life circumstances, working styles, and definitions of success.

Y: Yield to Collective Wisdom

This is the principle that makes all the others work.

Yielding to collective wisdom means accepting that the best solutions come from combining different perspectives rather than from any single viewpoint, no matter how expert. It means designing decision-making processes that integrate different voices, not just collect them.

The engineer who left had wisdom the company desperately needed. She knew what was broken. She knew how it felt. She knew what it cost. If someone had yielded to her perspective, listened and acted on what she was telling them, the company would have started its transformation years earlier instead of waiting until the pattern became undeniable.

The engineer who stayed contributed insights her team had been missing for years. Her thoughtful, deliberate style of analysis caught problems that quick verbal processing missed. When the team finally yielded to her way of working—made space for it rather than dismissing it—everyone's work improved.

On a House music dance floor, the DJ does not play their favorite track on repeat. They listen to the crowd. They feel the energy. They yield to the collective wisdom of the room about what the moment needs. The best sets emerge from this dialogue between DJ and dance floor, a conversation where both sides contribute and neither dominates.

In practice: Design decision-making processes that integrate different viewpoints. Create space for minority opinions to influence outcomes. Track whether diverse input actually changes decisions or just decorates them.

The Dance Floor in Practice

HARMONY is not a checklist. It is a design philosophy. You do not implement it once and move on. You practice it, the way a DJ practices reading the room, the way a musician practices their instrument.

The company did not become perfect after the redesign. No organization does. But the experience of working there changed fundamentally for people who had previously felt invisible. Engagement scores shifted. Retention improved. Innovation accelerated. And most importantly, people started showing up as themselves rather than performing a version of themselves they thought the culture required.

The exit interview that started everything was painful. But it was also a gift. One person's willingness to be heard, to tell the truth on her way out the door, created the opening for transformation that benefited everyone who came after her.

That is what belonging produces. Not just better experiences for individuals, but better outcomes for everyone. The music does sound better with all of us, not as a slogan, but as a measurable, demonstrable reality.

The Philosophy Beneath the Framework

I have given you HARMONY as a framework, because frameworks are useful. They provide language, structure, and a way to evaluate whether your efforts are working.

But HARMONY did not come from a vacuum. It came from a philosophy that transformed how I think about inclusion—one I encountered through a man whose work became the intellectual foundation for everything in this book.

I first encountered john a. powell (he spells his name in lowercase, a deliberate choice to express that he is not above others or the universe) through a virtual convening during the pandemic. john was on a mission to bring together CEOs and their chief diversity officers to transform the world of work, to create a future where belonging would be institutionalized and othering would be marginalized. One of my previous CEOs, who was already being mentored by john, invited me in.

I was already familiar with his framework of targeted universalism. I had read about it, referenced it in presentations, and understood it intellectually. But I had never heard the person who created it, or, as I came to think of it, *channeled* it, speak.

It sounds like something you might say about a spiritual experience because it was one. Even through a screen, the air felt different when he spoke. He embodied such wisdom, such deep connection to the work, that there was no way you could sit in that virtual room and not want to be part of whatever he was building. It was like hearing a sermon on a scripture you've heard many times from different pastors, but this one reached a soulful place in you that no other pastor had touched before.

When the Framework Found Its Home

What john gave me that day, and in every interaction since, was not just a theory. It was the design philosophy that made sense of everything I had been trying to do for twenty-five years.

Targeted universalism starts with a deceptively simple premise: Set universal goals that apply to everyone, then recognize that different groups are situated differently relative to those goals. Some groups face barriers that others do not. Some start closer to the goal; others start much further away. Some face structural, historical, economic, geographic, or cultural obstacles that identical treatment will never overcome.

The "targeted" part is the strategy. You develop different approaches for different groups based on how they are actually situated, not on how you assume they are situated. You meet people where they are, not where a one-size-fits-all program imagines them to be.

The "universal" part is the goal. Everyone reaches the same destination. Everyone belongs. Everyone thrives. The destination does not change; only the pathway changes, because the starting points are different based on who and where you are.

Think about what that means in practice. When Angela, the top-performing store manager from Chapter 5, was offered a promotion that would have been a pay cut, the universal goal was clear: Advance top talent into leadership. But Angela's starting point was different from the starting point the system assumed. She was a caregiver for multiple generations. She depended on performance bonuses the new role would eliminate. The standard promotion package, designed universally, would have produced an unequal outcome for her because it failed to account for how she was actually situated.

We practiced targeted universalism when we redesigned her package. The goal stayed universal: Advance this exceptional leader. The strategy became targeted: address her specific financial and logistical barriers so she could actually reach that goal.

When Muslim employees at the distribution centers were being written up for leaving the floor to pray, the universal goal was clear: Every employee performs at their best. The targeted strategy was equally clear: Create conditions—a designated prayer space, a predictable schedule, adequate coverage—that allowed those specific employees to meet that universal standard without sacrificing their religious identity to do it.

When we redesigned the tech company's meeting structures so that the quiet engineer could contribute, the universal goal was unchanged: Capture the best thinking from every team member. The targeted strategy, written brainstorming, reflection time, and asynchronous channels addressed the specific barrier she faced in a culture that only rewarded one style of participation.

This is not special treatment. This is intelligent design. It is the recognition that identical treatment in the context of different circumstances produces unequal outcomes, and that if you actually care about the universal goal, you have to be willing to vary the approach.

john's framework gave me language for what I had been doing intuitively and helped me do it with far greater precision. Every element of HARMONY is, at its core, an application of targeted universalism. Honoring different styles means recognizing that people are situated differently in how they communicate and contribute and then designing for that difference rather than ignoring it. Nurturing growth for everyone means understanding that career pathways that work for some create barriers for others, and then targeting your development strategies accordingly. Yielding to collective wisdom means acknowledging that no single perspective, no matter how expert, captures the full picture of how different groups experience the same system.

After learning to apply targeted universalism at an enterprise level from the source, it became the frame through which I wanted to design, deliver, and lead all of my work —not as an add-on to existing approaches, but as the foundational logic. You cannot build HARMONY without it. You cannot create belonging without asking: Who is situated differently, and what do they specifically need to reach the goal we all share?

When the Philosophy Had a Body

A few years later, my colleague Dr. Rachel Talton and I traveled to Berkeley to meet john in person. I had been learning from him virtually, absorbing his thinking and integrating targeted universalism into my practice. But nothing prepared me for the experience of being in his presence.

Rachel described what happened when she first hugged him: "I felt—it's ancestral. I looked at this man and I felt, my God, what an unbelievable human. And he hadn't even said anything yet."

Then he started talking. About starting the institute. About his work in South Africa, casually mentioning his collaboration with Nelson Mandela as if it were simply part of his journey. For him, it was. Every conversation, whether with a president or a stranger on the street, receives the same warmth, the same presence, the same full attention.

"You think about what it means to feel like the air accepts you," Rachel said afterward. "That the humans accept you, that the table and chairs accept you, that you are just accepted in this space, in this universe. He literally encapsulates that in a person. He makes you feel like you're the only person there."

That is what belonging feels like when it has a body.

I left that day feeling smarter, not just with frameworks and science, though john provided plenty of both, but with a feeling. And feelings matter. Rachel said she was improved by thirty-five percent, and while she was joking about the number, she was not joking about the experience.

What struck me most was the coherence between his philosophy and his presence. Targeted universalism is, at its heart, about seeing people as they actually are, as human beings situated in specific circumstances that deserve specific attention. john does not just theorize this. He lives it. Every person in his presence receives the full weight of his attention, calibrated to who they are and what they need in that moment. He is the living practice of his own framework.

The question I have carried since that day: How do we take what he embodies into every space we occupy? How do we create organizations where people feel the way we felt in his presence, accepted by the air itself?

HARMONY is my attempt to translate that feeling into practice, powered by the design philosophy of targeted universalism. But frameworks alone do not create belonging. People do. Leaders who make others feel like they are the only person in the room. Colleagues who communicate

"You are accepted here" through their presence, not just their policies. Systems that say "You belong" through their design, not just their mission statements.

Belonging is not just something we build. It is something we become.

The dance floor is built. The music is playing. People are not just included; they belong.

In the next chapter, we will step back and see the whole house we have been building. The promised land is not a destination. It is a way of seeing.

Chapter 8
Promised Land
The Vision

Take me to the promised land.

— Joe Smooth, "Promised Land"

Every builder needs to know what they are building toward. Not just the next wall or the next room, but the completed house. The vision of what it will mean to live there.

This chapter is the vision. Stepping back from the construction to see the World House as it could be. Not perfect, not complete, but real. A place where the promised land that Joe Smooth sang about becomes possible, not through escape, but through building.

The promised land is not a place you find. It is a place you make.

When Everything Comes Together

It was 1987 when Joe Smooth released "Promised Land," a track that captured the hope and longing of an entire community reaching for something better. The song was not just about individual dreams. It was about collective transformation, about building the kind of world where everyone could thrive.

I have spent twenty-five years building rooms in the World House. Some were constructed under ideal conditions with supportive leadership and adequate resources. Others were built during storms, in hostile environments, with people actively trying to tear down what we were putting up. I have seen brilliant efforts fail because the infrastructure could not hold them. I have seen modest changes transform entire cultures because they were planted in the right soil.

Now I want to step back and show you what the completed house looks like, not as an abstraction, but as a composite of the best I have witnessed across every organization I have had the privilege to lead.

No single company got everything right. But each one taught me something about what becomes possible when belonging is real. Together, they form a picture of what we are building toward.

The Organization I Have Seen

I have seen what happens when a leader stops asking "How do we fix our diversity numbers?" and starts asking "How do we build a place where everyone belongs?" The shift seems subtle, but it changes everything.

In the organization I have seen, hiring managers do not evaluate candidates against an unspoken template of who has always succeeded here. They ask what this person will bring that we do not already have. The job description means what it says. The criteria that are stated are the criteria that are applied. And when a manager's gut feeling diverges from the evidence, there is a system that catches it, not to punish, but to pause and examine.

In the organization I have seen, a top-performing store manager is not punished for having a life that does not match the assumptions of the people who designed the promotion structure. When Angela hesitated about advancement, someone asked why and then redesigned the package so she could succeed on her own terms. That redesign did not just help Angela. It revealed how many other high performers had been quietly opting out because the pathway was never built for them.

In the organization I have seen, Muslim employees on a distribution center floor are not written up for observing their faith. A ten-minute prayer break and a designated room transform them from employees who feel surveilled into employees who feel seen. Productivity does not suffer. It improves. Because employees who know their employer cares about what they need give back more than employees who are just trying to survive their shift.

In the organization I have seen, a brilliant engineer who processes information quietly is not mistaken for someone who has nothing to say. The meeting has been redesigned with written components, reflection time, and multiple channels for contribution, so that her thoughtful analysis reaches the team instead of being drowned out by whoever speaks fastest. She stays. She advances. She becomes one of the most valuable contributors on her team. Not because she changed, but because the system learned to recognize her.

In the organization I have seen, employee resource groups are not decorative. They have budgets, accountability, and seats at the table where key business decisions are made. When they bring customer insights that the marketing team never considered, those insights shape what gets built. Revenue grows in markets that had been written off. Innovation accelerates because the range of perspectives informing decisions finally reflects the range of people being served.

In the organization I have seen, an executive who started as the most resistant person in the room ends up marching in a Pride parade, not because he was shamed into it, but because someone planted a seed with patience and data and respect, and it grew into something no one could have predicted.

In the organization I have seen, when a talented engineer walks out the door and tells the truth about why she is leaving, the response is not to coach the next person to tolerate the same conditions. The response is to rebuild the systems that failed her, including standardized pay, transparent advancement criteria, and HR partners trained to recognize patterns of exclusion, so that the next engineer with her talent stays and thrives.

None of these are hypothetical. I witnessed every one of them. They happened in different companies, in different industries, in different decades of my career. But they share a common thread: Someone decided that the way things had always been done was not good enough. Someone asked who this system is *not* working for. Someone had the courage to redesign.

That is the promised land. Not perfection. Not the absence of conflict or the elimination of bias, but the presence of systems, leaders, and cultures that are actively oriented toward seeing every person fully and creating the conditions for them to contribute their best.

The World I Want to Build

I want to tell you what I believe.

I believe every person is worthy of love in all the ways love presents itself: dignity, respect, opportunity, care, attention, grace.

I believe we should see each other the way we see babies. When you look at a newborn, you do not see limitations. You see inherent beauty. You handle that child with care. You see limitless potential and possibility. You do not ask what that baby has done to earn your tenderness. The tenderness is the default.

I am not suggesting we infantilize anyone. I am suggesting the opposite. What if we empowered people through that same orientation, through the fundamental belief that every human being arrives with value, and that our job is to create conditions where that value can be fully expressed?

Not earned. Not proven. Not extracted through performance reviews and promotion committees and cultures that demand people contort themselves into someone else's template before they are deemed worthy.

Expressed. Freely. Because the systems were designed to let it happen.

That is what Dr. King was building toward when he wrote of the World House. Not a house where everyone is the same, but a house where everyone is seen. Where difference is not a problem to be managed but a resource to be honored. Where the family that is unduly separated in ideas, culture, and interest learns to live together, not by erasing those differences, but by building structures that hold them all.

That is what john powell channels when he speaks of belonging. The experience of being accepted by the air itself. Not conditionally. Not after you have proven your worth. Accepted as you arrive.

That is what House music has been practicing on dance floors for forty years: every style of movement welcome;

every body belonging. The only credential required is your willingness to be present.

And that is what targeted universalism makes operationally possible. You set the universal goal, everyone belongs, everyone thrives, everyone contributes their best, and then you do the honest, rigorous, creative work of understanding how different people are situated relative to that goal and what each group specifically needs to reach it.

The vision is not complicated. It is demanding. It requires us to believe something simple and act on it relentlessly: Every person is worth being fully seen.

For Those Who Were Displaced

I need to speak directly now to a specific community. To the more than 300,000 practitioners—many of them Black women, many of them trans, many of them people who gave their careers to this work in corporate, government, nonprofit, and educational settings—who have been displaced. Pushed out. Defunded. Told that the work they dedicated their professional lives to was not just unnecessary but harmful.

I see you.

I know what it cost you to do this work. Not just the professional investment, the degrees, the certifications, the decades of expertise, but the personal cost. The emotional labor of being the person in the room who names the uncomfortable truth. The exhaustion of building programs that transform cultures, only to watch them be dismantled by the next administration or the next CEO or the next news cycle. The particular sting of being punished for doing exactly what you were hired to do.

You were not wrong. The work was not wrong. The skills you developed—cultural competence, organizational design, facilitation, conflict resolution, systems thinking, human development—are not relics of a trend. They are leadership competencies that every organization on earth needs, whether they call it DEI or not.

So, here is my vision for where we go and what we do now.

First, we find each other. We create community. Not out of nostalgia for what was, but out of recognition that our collective intellect, experience, and resources are too valuable to scatter. We convene. We coalesce. We build networks that sustain us and sharpen our practice.

Second, we evolve. The field needed this reckoning; not the cruelty of it, but the honesty it forced. Some of what was built after 2020 was performative. Some of it was disconnected from business reality. Some of it repeated approaches that had already been tried and evolved from decades earlier. We know this. We said it before the backlash made it convenient for others to say it. Now we have the opportunity to rebuild the practice on a stronger foundation, anchored in the metrics, the cultural competence frameworks, the systems-level thinking that this work always required.

Third, we go where the work is valued. There are companies around the world, not just in the United States, that understand the competitive advantage of cultures where everyone belongs. There are leaders who know that homogeneous teams have blind spots they cannot see, that markets are diverse and growing more so, and that the organizations winning the war for talent differentiate themselves through culture and opportunity. Those leaders need us. Our expertise is not diminished because one country's political moment has declared it inconvenient.

Fourth, we become the bridge builders this book has been describing. Not waiting for organizations to hire us back into roles with DEI in the title, but embedding our skills into every context we enter: consulting, coaching, advising, leading, teaching, building businesses of our own. Cultural competence is not a department. It is a capability. And we carry it with us wherever we go.

The displacement is real. The pain is real. But so is this truth: *They would not have dismantled this work so aggressively if it were not working.* You do not tear down what is ineffective. You tear down what is threatening. And belonging is threatening to anyone who profits from separation.

We are still here. The work is still here. And the world still needs what we know how to build.

When the World Tells You to Stop

The current environment presents a challenge unlike any I have seen in my career.

Every day brings new executive orders, policy reversals, and public attacks on the very concept of inclusion. A recent example crystallized the absurdity for me: The State Department announced it would no longer use Calibri font in official documents, declaring it a policy of the previous administration.

The actual history is instructive. The shift to Calibri happened because the font is easier to read for people with vision disabilities. It was an accessibility accommodation, a small change that helped some people without inconveniencing anyone else. Now it has been reversed under the premise that Times New Roman is more professional, with the subtext that accommodating people with disabilities somehow harms everyone else.

This is the logic we are up against. Inclusion is reframed as exclusion. Expanding opportunity is characterized as taking something away. Creating space for everyone is portrayed as an attack on those who already had space.

Organizations I work with are navigating confusion. Even leaders who recognize that inclusion drives business results, that diverse teams innovate more effectively, that belonging improves retention and performance—even those leaders are asking whether they should continue. Whether it is safe. Whether the risk is worth it.

My advice has not changed. But my framing has.

Start With Values, Not Labels

Every organization has stated values. Integrity. Excellence. Customer focus. Opportunity for all. Innovation. Respect.

The conversation I have with leaders begins there. What do your values actually mean? And is everyone in your organization experiencing those values fully?

If you value customer service, are all your customers receiving excellent service? Or are some populations having worse experiences because your employees do not know how to engage across difference?

If you value hiring the best talent, are you actually accessing the full talent marketplace? Or do your recruiting practices only reach certain networks, certain schools, certain backgrounds?

If you value innovation, do you hear from the full range of perspectives in your organization? Or are some voices systematically excluded from the conversations where ideas are generated and decisions are made?

This reframing removes the false dichotomy that has poisoned the discourse. The question is not whether you focus on marginalized groups or on merit. The question is whether your stated values translate into lived experience for everyone.

When there is a gap between what you say and what people experience, you have work to do. You do not need to call it DEI. You do not need to use any particular language. You need to align your practices with your principles.

What the Resistance Reveals

The backlash against inclusion work often operates on an unstated assumption: that opportunities for historically excluded groups come at the expense of historically included groups. That the pie is fixed, and any slice given to others is taken from someone else.

Underneath that assumption is another one, rarely spoken aloud: that certain people are inherently more qualified, more deserving, more naturally suited for opportunity. That when we expand access, we are lowering standards rather than expanding our recognition of excellence.

This is the belief that has to be named and examined. The perception of inherent qualification for all opportunities, held by those who have always had access, is not evidence of actual superior qualification. It is evidence of a system that was designed to recognize and reward people who look and sound a certain way.

I once read about the Irish potato famine, where a country dependent on the potato as its primary food source almost faced extinction when their only variety of potato was plagued with blight, a form of parasitic infestation. That famine resulted in the deaths of more than one million people and the forced migration of approximately two million more. The Mayan region of the Americas depended on the potato for food as well; however, they cultivated many different potato varieties that acted as a shield when disease struck. That biodiversity preserved their food supply for generations.

These examples shine a light on a simple truth: Sustained homogeneity, whether in who leads or who benefits, is a recipe for destruction. Going forward, organizations that thrive will be those that understand this. The rest create cultures that only work for some people and lose the talent of everyone else. The hubris of believing you already have access to the best thinking, the best talent, the best ideas creates risks that no amount of confidence can overcome. Sameness will miss opportunities that only difference can find.

The businesses that create something new, that generate the innovation and growth that define the next era, will be the ones that cultivate diversity of perspective and create cultures in which that difference can thrive.

I have no interest in playing rhetorical games with those who argue in bad faith. But I will say plainly what I believe: inclusion is not a political position. It is a recognition of reality. The world is diverse. Customers are diverse. Talent is diverse. Organizations that cannot effectively engage that diversity will be outcompeted by those that can.

The question is not whether to do this work. The question is whether you will do it thoughtfully, strategically, and with the courage to persist when the environment makes it difficult.

You have seen the vision. You know what we are building toward. Not a perfect world, but an honest one. A world where every person is seen the way we see a child: with inherent worth, handled with care, and full of possibility. A world where systems are designed to let that possibility flourish rather than contain it.

In the final chapter, you will cross the threshold from reader to builder. You will make the choice about what role you will play in constructing the World House.

Chapter 9
On and On
The Threshold

House music is a universal language that speaks to the soul. It doesn't matter where you come from, what you look like, or who you love. When that beat drops, we're all one family.

> — Vince Lawrence, House Music pioneer and producer of "On and On"

You have walked through every room. Now you stand at the threshold.

The threshold is the boundary between inside and outside, the place where the World House meets the world that still needs building. This chapter is for the bridge builders, the ones who will carry this work beyond any single organization or community and into every space they occupy.

The beat does not stop when the party ends. It goes on and on. The work of building the World House is not a project with a completion date. It is a practice, a rhythm, a way of moving through the world that continues as long as you do.

You are not the last builder. You are a link in the lineage. And what you carry forward matters.

The Rhythm That Continues

It is late on a Saturday night in a Chicago warehouse, sometime in the mid-1980s. The DJ has been reading the crowd all evening, building energy, working through resistance, creating moments where strangers found their common rhythm. Now, as the night reaches its peak, something is happening on that dance floor that logic cannot fully explain.

People who walked in alone are moving together. The banker dances next to the factory worker. The college student learns steps from someone's grandmother. The person who was too scared to dance at the beginning of the night is now in the center of the floor, surrounded by encouragers. Different styles, different backgrounds, different stories, all contributing to one incredible, unrepeatable moment of collective joy.

This is what we have been building toward. Not a program or a policy, but a way of being together that makes this kind of magic possible.

And the question at the threshold is this: What happens when the night ends and everyone goes home?

The answer, the only answer that matters, is that they carry the rhythm with them. Into their workplaces. Into their families. Into every room they enter. The beat does not stop because the party is over. It goes on and on, in the bodies and choices of the people who felt it.

That is what this chapter is about. Not what you learned in this book, but what you do with it when you step outside these pages.

The Most Resistant Room I Ever Entered

For this story I'm going to name the company. Not to expose or critique, but to speak my truth as I experienced it. And to show how the work continues.

The most resistance I ever encountered was at L Brands.

For those unfamiliar, L Brands was a Fortune 500 retail conglomerate that housed some of the most recognizable consumer brands in the world: Victoria's Secret, Bath & Body Works, Pink, and others, all under one corporate umbrella headquartered in Columbus, Ohio. At its peak, the company was a retail empire. Victoria's Secret alone was a cultural force, its annual fashion show drawing millions of viewers and defining mainstream beauty standards for decades.

I was recruited to help transform the company's culture following a high-profile incident where a customer had been racially profiled in one of the Victoria's Secret stores. The incident was recorded, went viral, and resulted in a lawsuit that made national news. The company's response was to bring in someone who could work across brands to address the deeper cultural issues the incident had revealed.

During my interviews, I heard all the right things. Leaders spoke passionately about wanting to transform the culture, about being intentional with inclusion, about ensuring that customers from all backgrounds felt welcomed. It sounded like exactly the mandate I was hoping for.

The reality I encountered was something different entirely.

L Brands was highly fractured. Each brand operated with significant autonomy, developing its own culture and practices independently. The corporate center was pushing toward more centralization, but the incentive structures had not caught up. Brand leaders were rewarded based on their individual brand's performance, not on collaboration across the enterprise. There was no structural motivation for anyone to embrace strategies coming from the center, including mine.

Victoria's Secret presented the most intense resistance. And the brand was already facing an existential reckoning that had nothing to do with me but with other brands in their space. Savage X Fenty had arrived with a business model built explicitly on inclusivity, celebrating every body type, expanding every definition of beauty, reaching customers Victoria's Secret had never considered relevant. Aerie was gaining market share with unretouched campaigns. After decades of unchallenged dominance, Victoria's Secret was losing ground to competitors who were using inclusion as their competitive differentiator.

My team came to them with ideas for exactly this kind of transformation. We proposed expanding product ranges to reflect diverse customers. We suggested incorporating more diversity into the Victoria's Secret Fashion Show. We developed learning content for store associates. We designed engagement workshops. We brought proposal after proposal showing how inclusivity could become a business advantage rather than a threat.

Everything was rejected.

"This would never work." "This is not who we are." "Clearly you do not understand our brand and our business."

The resistance was not just rejection. It was dismissal. Our work was framed as a distraction from the real business, as something that would dilute rather than strengthen the brand.

Then a senior creative leader gave a now-infamous interview with Vogue in which he dismissed the possibility of featuring transgender models or more diverse body types in the Fashion Show, essentially declaring that the brand already knew what its customers wanted. The reaction was immediate and devastating. Social media erupted. High-profile brand ambassadors publicly distanced themselves. The controversy compounded the already mounting business challenges. Within months, the Fashion Show, long considered the most-watched fashion event in the world, was canceled.

None of us inside the company were surprised. The executive had simply said publicly what the culture had been communicating privately all along.

Building in Resistant Soil

I tried multiple approaches to break through.

I proposed making DEI learning mandatory across the enterprise. Rejected immediately.

So I focused on what I could influence. The employee resource groups at L Brands, when I arrived, were informal social networks disconnected from any business strategy: no alignment with talent goals, no measurable outcomes, no budgets. Working with my team, we redesigned them as Inclusion Resource Groups with direct connections to business priorities, defined outcomes, allocated budgets, and linked to employee engagement metrics. We opened membership to all employees, not just those from under-represented groups. This approach worked. We built a grassroots foundation that demonstrated the business value of inclusion through tangible results.

I tried working brand by brand since the centralized approach was not gaining traction. The results were mixed. Pink's leadership understood that their younger demographic already expected inclusion; it was a purchase driver for that customer, not a nice-to-have. We made real progress there. Bath & Body Works had leaders who understood the stakes of this work and were receptive. But Victoria's Secret leadership remained largely closed.

We did achieve some wins even there. We got senior leaders to participate in company-wide inclusion content. We secured time at major leadership meetings to conduct workshops. We cascaded virtual learning into the stores. It was not enough to fundamentally transform a culture that had decades of momentum behind it, but it was enough to plant seeds.

We also built something I am especially proud of: deep partnerships with Historically Black Colleges and Universities. We created talent pipelines that gave students at schools like Howard and Spelman real career pathways into the company. We brought a mobile retail experience to a 2,000-student HBCU campus, and it outsold retail activations at universities ten times that size. That was not charity. That was proof of concept, evidence that the customers and talent the brand had been overlooking represented enormous untapped potential.

Then L Brands dissolved, splitting Victoria's Secret and Bath & Body Works into separate publicly traded companies.

What the Seeds Became

I was not there to see what happened next. But here is what I know.

The Inclusion Resource Groups we built continued. They still hold annual summits. They still represent those brands at community events and celebrations. The learning content stayed in place. The HBCU relationships continued to produce diverse talent pipelines. Students at those campuses now see career pathways that did not exist before we showed up.

The stores still use language and design elements my team created. The infrastructure we built became part of how those organizations operated, not because anyone was championing it from the top, but because it was embedded deeply enough in systems and processes that removing it would have been harder than keeping it.

And in 2023, the Victoria's Secret Fashion Show returned. This time, it featured the most diverse cast in its history: different body types, different backgrounds, different definitions of beauty. The very transformation that had been rejected when my team proposed it had become the brands new identity.

I do not take sole credit for that evolution. Culture change is never the work of one person, and the market forces that ultimately pushed Victoria's Secret toward inclusion were powerful and multidirectional. But I know that the foundation we built, the frameworks we embedded into systems, the relationships we cultivated, and the seeds we planted in the most resistant soil I have ever encountered contributed to what those brands eventually became.

Sometimes transformation does not happen on your timeline. Sometimes you do the work knowing you will not be there to see it bear fruit. But you do it anyway, because what you build into infrastructure will outlast any individual leader's resistance.

That is the legacy of this work, even when resistance comes from every direction. You may not win every battle. You may not transform every heart. But if you build inclusion into systems, into processes, into the operational architecture of an organization, it becomes harder to remove than any opponent imagined.

When You Are the Bridge to a Community You Harmed

Sometimes the hardest conversations are not about defending your own beliefs. They are about representing an organization that has done real damage to a community you care about.

After that senior creative leader's interview went viral, one of the public figures who spoke out mentioned a specific nonprofit organization that supported a community that the leader's comments had directly harmed. The company wanted to offer a significant donation to the nonprofit and asked me to deliver it in person.

I did not want to do it. I put myself in the shoes of that nonprofit's leadership and imagined how I would feel if someone from this company showed up at my door with a check. It would look like we were trying to buy our way out of accountability, to purchase absolution rather than earn it.

But I made the trip because it was the right thing to do, even if it was being done for complicated reasons.

I prepared differently for this conversation than I had for any other in my career. I knew that going in with a defensive posture would confirm every negative assumption they had about the company. I knew that leading with the donation would make it feel transactional rather than relational. I knew that this conversation was not really about the money.

So, I decided to lead with listening.

I went in prepared to present the donation, but more importantly, I went in prepared to create space for whatever feedback they needed to give. My intention was not to defend or deny but to acknowledge that harm had been done and to present myself and the company as seeking to learn and grow, rather than trying to take the stink off its name.

The conversation was difficult. There were hurt feelings and hard feedback. The nonprofits leaders did not hold back about the damage that had been done, about the real impact on the community they served, people who already faced enough challenges without seeing a major brand's leader dismissing their existence on a national platform.

I listened to all of it. I did not interrupt to explain or justify. I did not offer context that might minimize the impact. I acknowledged the harm and asked what would be most helpful moving forward, as an ally rather than a company seeking quick absolution.

I think my approach helped. I cannot claim that it repaired all the damage or that the organization walked away with a positive view of the brand. But I believe I gave them something different from what they expected: a representative who was willing to hear their pain without defensiveness, who acknowledged the legitimacy of their anger, and who was asking how to do better rather than just writing a check and walking away.

Sometimes that is the work: not achieving perfect outcomes, but creating moments where a different future becomes possible. Planting seeds of trust in soil that has been poisoned by harm. Holding space for pain, while keeping the door open to healing.

Bridge-building is not always about connecting people who are merely different. Sometimes it is about connecting people who have been hurt to the institutions that caused the hurt. And the bridge builder stands in the middle, holding both truths: This organization failed this community, *and* this organization can learn to do better.

That is the hardest place to stand. It is also the most necessary.

What You Carry Forward

If you have been practicing the ideas in this book, even imperfectly, even in small ways, you have already become something powerful: a bridge builder in a world that desperately needs more connectors.

You are no longer just someone who supports inclusion as an idea. You have seen the "Diversity Distortions" that build walls, and you know how to name them without shaming the people who hold them. You have practiced the listening skills that make connection possible across difference. You understand what moves people off the sidelines: not guilt, not lectures, but patience and data and respect planted like seeds that grow on their own timeline.

You have learned to lead from the DJ booth, guiding without controlling, creating conditions for collective contribution rather than demanding conformity. You know that trust requires benevolence, competence, and integrity working together, and that psychological safety is the enabler of all three.

You have seen what broken infrastructure produces—the hiring manager who overrides his own criteria, the promotion that punishes someone for having a different life—and you know that good intentions without good systems produce bad outcomes. You know that targeted universalism is not special treatment, but intelligent design: universal goals, targeted strategies, equitable outcomes.

You have walked the dance floor where HARMONY operates, where different styles are honored, unique contributions are appreciated, power rotates, authentic relationships form, shared purpose organizes, growth is nurtured for everyone, and collective wisdom guides decisions.

And you know that belonging is not just something we build. It is something we become.

Most importantly, you understand that this work is not about being perfect or having all the answers. It is about being committed to growth, connection, and justice. It is about showing up consistently, learning from mistakes, and staying engaged even when progress feels slow or the environment turns hostile.

The threshold is before you. Behind you is everything you have learned. Before you is everything you might build.

What you build matters. Who you include matters. How you show up matters.

The World House is not finished. It may never be finished. But it grows larger with every person who decides to be a builder rather than a bystander.

Epilogue: The World House

You have walked through every room.

You have learned to demolish the myths that divide us. You have studied the blueprint of empathetic understanding. You have joined the crew mobilizing against resistance. You have entered the DJ booth and learned to lead as a guide rather than a gatekeeper. You have laid infrastructure that makes belonging sustainable. You have poured the foundation, honoring the history we stand on. You have built the dance floor where everyone belongs. You have framed the windows facing a promised land of resilient connection. You have crossed the threshold where bridge builders carry this work into the world.

Now you stand at the door.

And I want to take you to one more place before you walk through it.

The Second Saturday in July

Every year, on the second Saturday in July, something happens in Chicago that most of the world does not know about.

Tens of thousands of people descend upon Jackson Park on the South Side—the same South Side where I grew up, where my grandmother raised foster children and my grandfather worked the polls, the same streets I walked listening to House music on my headphones. They come from across the city, across the country, across the world. They bring coolers and lawn chairs and blankets. They bring their children and their parents. They bring friends they have danced with for decades and strangers they will dance with for the first time.

It is the Chosen Few Picnic and Festival, and it is the longest-running House music festival on earth.

The Chosen Few DJs—Wayne Williams, Jesse Saunders, Tony Hatchett, Alan King, and Andre Hatchett—have been playing together since the early 1980s. They were there at the beginning. They watched Frankie Knuckles build something holy at the Warehouse. I followed these guys all around town to hear them spin: The Power Plant, Sauer's, The Riviera, Dejoie's. Their music was the soundtrack of my youth, and they became the keepers of a sound that the rest of the world would eventually come looking for.

The festival itself started the way all House music starts, from nothing, with everything. In the early 1990s, those five DJs set up in the grassy area behind the Museum of

Science and Industry in Jackson Park. No stage. No sponsors. No permits. Just turntables, speakers, a few crates of records, and an invitation to friends: come through, we are going to play some music and have some fun.

That is it. That is how the longest-running House music festival on earth began. A handful of DJs and their people, doing what they had always done: creating space, building community, letting the music hold everyone together.

Word spread the way it always does in House culture, through the grapevine, through the feeling, through the people who showed up once and could not stay away. The crowd grew. The park filled. What started as a cookout with a soundtrack became a pilgrimage. And those DJs never stopped. They kept playing when House music left Chicago and conquered the world but somehow forgot to come home. They kept playing when the city pushed back on permits, when the mainstream moved on to the next thing, when a thousand forces conspired to make them quit.

They kept playing.

And every July, the world comes back to them.

I started going regularly after college in the late nineties. It was a great excuse to hear my favorite music, see old friends, and hang out in my favorite city park, which happened to be directly across from my high school. But what kept me coming back, year after year, was not nostalgia. It was the feeling.

I want to tell you what that feeling is, because the feeling is the point.

You arrive and the music is already playing. You can hear it before you can see the park, that bass vibrating through the trees the same way it reached through the walls of Mendel High School when I was eleven years old. As you get closer, the crowd comes into view, and it takes your breath away—not because of the size, though the size is staggering. Because of the composition.

There are seventy-year-old women in sundresses dancing with the same precision and joy they brought to the Warehouse in 1978. There are teenagers discovering this sound for the first time, looking around with the same wide eyes I had in that gymnasium. There are white couples from the suburbs who found House music through the global electronic scene and traced it back to its source. There are Japanese tourists who flew to Chicago specifically for this weekend. There are families, actual families, three generations deep, sharing a blanket and a groove.

There are hundreds of white tents, each one representing a cherished connection. A fraternity or sorority. A neighborhood block club. Alumni groups. Contingents from cities across the country. Each one creates its own vibe, like tailgating to a groove, all decked out with every amenity for the groups to enjoy the full day together. I can never commit to one spot, so I can be found floating from tent to tent, reconnecting with old friends, classmates, co-workers, church members, all across the park over our shared love of the music.

But I am there to dance. Not because I have killer moves, but because that is what the sound compels me to do. Nobody is checking credentials. Nobody is asking where you came from or what you do for a living or who you voted for. The music does not care. It never has. The only question the dance floor asks is: Are you willing to be here?

The dance floor at Chosen Few is a massive open grassy area in front of the main stage. The space fills from a few dozen in the morning to a peak of maybe five to seven thousand by late afternoon, and the energy builds with it. You would think with that many people in such close proximity there would be issues. Fights. Crime. Bad behavior. Not here. Chosen Few is hallowed ground. This is a place of joy, of unity, or as one person put it, "This is what freedom looks like."

I watch Alan King work the crowd and I see everything this book has been trying to teach. He reads the room, all fifty thousand of it, the way a great leader reads an organization. He knows when to push the energy and when to let the crowd breathe. He drops a track that the old heads recognize and the roar that goes up is not just nostalgia— it is testimony. *We were here. We built this. It survived everything that tried to kill it.* Then he blends in something new, something the younger dancers lock onto immediately, and for a few bars both generations are moving to the same beat without either one compromising.

That is HARMONY. That is targeted universalism in 4/4

time. That is the World House with grass under its feet and sun on its shoulders.

And here is what touches my soul every single time. Somewhere around late afternoon, when the sun starts going golden and the music has been building for hours, that peak time when the dance floor is the most full, there is a moment. You cannot plan it. You cannot manufacture it. The entire park seems to synchronize. Tens of thousands of people—strangers and lovers and families and people who just wandered in off the street—all moving together. Not the same moves. Not the same style. But the same feeling. The same surrender to something larger than any one of them.

For that moment, there is no division. There is no back-lash. There is no political argument about whether belonging is worth building. There is just the undeniable, felt experience of what it means to be part of something that holds all of you, not despite your differences, but through them.

That is what we are building toward. That feeling. At scale. In organizations and communities and nations.

I know it is possible because I have felt it. Every July. On the South Side of Chicago. On the same ground where my grandmother taught me that community is daily practice and my grandfather taught me that democracy is a right worth fighting for.

The Chosen Few have been proving it for over thirty years. The beat did not stop when the mainstream walked away.

It did not stop when the city said no. It did not stop when the original DJs got older, because they raised a next generation who understood that the music was never really about the music. It was about what happens between people when the conditions are right.

That is the legacy. Not a festival. A proof of concept.

The World House is not theoretical. I have stood in it. I have danced in it. It is real.

In 1967, Dr. Martin Luther King Jr. wrote of the World House the inescapable truth that we have inherited a large house, a great World House in which we must live together. Black and white, Easterner and Westerner, Gentile and Jew, Catholic and Protestant, Muslim and Hindu. A family unduly separated in ideas, culture, and interest who, because we can never again live apart, must learn somehow to live with each other in peace.

Nearly sixty years later, we are still learning. And some of us have stopped trying.

The world is fracturing. Division is no longer a byproduct; it is a strategy. Structures designed to bring us together are being dismantled, not because they failed, but because they worked. Because belonging is threatening to those who profit from separation. Because when people find each other across difference, they become harder to control.

In boardrooms and statehouses, the word inclusion has become a liability. Hundreds of thousands of practitioners, the architects of belonging, have been displaced, demoted, erased. More than 300,000 people have lost their jobs in a single year, casualties of policies designed to punish those who dared to build bridges. The message is clear: Go back to your corners. Stay in your lane. Stop reaching for each other.

We reject this.

Not with naivety. Not with denial of real challenges. But with the stubborn insistence that what we have seen is possible is worth fighting for.

Because we have seen it.

We have seen what happens when a company stops asking, "How do we fix our diversity numbers?" and starts asking, "How do we build a place where everyone belongs?" We have watched the metrics shift, not because someone mandated it, but because belonging creates performance.

We have seen a general counsel who spent his career managing risk become a fierce advocate for inclusion, because the stakes were personal.

We have seen ERGs transform from support groups into business partners, creating products that resonated with customers who had never before seen themselves reflected in what a company made.

We have seen a store manager who could not afford a promotion help redesign advancement systems so that talent would no longer be lost to assumptions that only fit some people's lives.

We have stood in spaces where belonging was not a program but an atmosphere, where the air itself seemed to accept you.

We have danced with fifty thousand strangers on the South Side of Chicago and known—not believed, *known*—that this is what the World House feels like when someone has the courage to build it.

We have seen what is possible. And we refuse to unsee it.

The Choice

There are people working to build the World House. And there are people working to tear it down.

The tearers have power right now. They have budgets and platforms and the momentum of backlash. They have the advantage of simplicity: It is always easier to destroy than to create, easier to divide than to bridge, easier to say "no" than to build "yes."

But they do not have the numbers. They do not have history. And they do not have the music.

We do not overcome resistance by fighting it directly. We overcome it by creating something so compelling, so life-giving, so undeniably better that people cannot help but move toward it.

We build the beat. We make the space. We let the music do what it has always done: bring people together across every line that is supposed to divide them.

The Invitation

The door to the World House is open.

It does not matter where you start from. It does not matter if you have been on the sidelines, or skeptical, or even part of tearing things down. The door is open to anyone ready to pick up a hammer and build.

Building looks different for everyone. Maybe you are a CEO who can reshape an entire organization. Maybe you are a manager who can change the experience of ten people. Maybe you are someone with no title at all who can shift a single conversation from division toward connection.

The World House is not constructed by heroes. It is constructed by ordinary people who decide, again and again, to do the next right thing. To listen when it would be easier to dismiss. To reach across when it would be safer to stay separate. To keep building when the structures are being dismantled around them.

That is the invitation. Not to be perfect. Not to have all the answers. Just to be a builder.

The Beat Must Go On

And now it goes on with you.

What you build matters. Who you include matters. How you show up matters.

The World House is not finished. It may never be finished. But it grows larger with every person who decides to be a builder rather than a bystander.

In the beginning, there was Jack.

And Jack had a groove.

And from this groove came the groove of all grooves.

The World House is waiting. The music is playing. The door is open.

You are ready.

Step through.

Discography

Please check out these tracks featured in The Beat Must Go On:

- Chip E., *Jack Trax*, House Mirage Records, 1985.
- Clivillés and Cole, "A Deeper Love," Columbia Records, 1991.
- Doctor's Cat, "Feel the Drive," ZYX Music, 1984.
- Fingers Inc., "Bring Down the Walls," Alleviated Records, Select Records, 1985.
- Inner City, "Good Life," Virgin, 1988.
- Jesse Saunders, "On and On," Jes Say Records, 1984.
- Joe Smooth, "Promised Land," DJ International, 1987.
- Loose Joints, "Is It All Over My Face," West End Records, 1980.
- Marshall Jefferson, "Move Your Body," Trax Records, 1986.
- Rhythm Controll with Chuck Roberts, "My House," Catch A Beat Records, 1987.
- Stardust, "Music Sounds Better with You," Roulé, 1998.

About the Author

Nichole Barnes Marshall discovered the principles of belonging on a Chicago dance floor before she ever had corporate language for them. Growing up on the South Side, she found House music at eleven years old—and spent the next three decades translating what she learned in those underground spaces into strategies that transform how organizations think about culture, talent, and inclusion.

With over 25 years leading human capital and culture transformation across six industries, including Chief

Diversity Officer roles at Pinterest, Bath & Body Works, and Aon, Nichole has built cultures that drive revenue growth, transform employee engagement, and outlast the leaders who resist change. She is the Founder and Chief Strategist of Marshall Matters, LLC, where she helps executives build organizations where people and business thrive together.

Nichole and her husband Kenny, a DJ, share a collection of over 20,000 vinyl, CD and digital records, a deep reverence for the artists who kept the beat alive, and an unshakeable belief that the most innovative ideas emerge when everyone in the room can dance in their own style. They live outside Detroit with their three children Kennedy, Erin, Nick and an adorable goldendoodle named Daisy.

www.ingramcontent.com/pod-product-compliance
Lightning Source LLC
Chambersburg PA
CBHW052359030726
47599CB00014B/1136